CORE CALLING

How to Build a Business that Gives You a Freedom Lifestyle in 2 Years or Less!

Shanda Sumpter

Published by Dignity Publishing

Printed in the United States of America.

ISBN 978-1514767399

This publication is designed to provide accurate and authoritative information with regard to the subject matter covered. It is sold with the understanding that the publisher is not engaged in rendering legal, accounting, or other professional advice. If legal advice or other expert assistance is required, the services of a competent professional should be sought. The opinions expressed by the authors in this book are not endorsed by Dignity Publishing and are the sole responsibility of the author rendering the opinion.

Most Dignity Publishing titles are available at special quantity discounts for bulk purchases for sales promotions, premiums, fundraising, and educational use. Special versions or book excerpts can also be created to fit specific needs.

◆

CONTENTS

◆

INTRODUCTION

The model of building a business that is used in today's world is antiquated. Many people still assume that you have to give up the time you want to spend with your family, your friends, and your fitness to be a successful entrepreneur. That is not true.

I have coached more than 2,000 people in many different fields of business, and I have found that there is a better way to build your business. After having tested this new approach to building a successful business for approximately five years, I have seen the results it yields. For that reason, I feel obligated to offer this information to you. Now is the time to stop burnout and start accessing true freedom!

The old model says that you are lucky if you make any money the first year of running your business, and you have to work hard to get it off the ground. The approach that I have been using for the past five years has proven that to be incorrect. Even if you have not perfected a plan or do not know what you want to sell, you can start a business. You can build an audience, sell to that audience, and take your business to a position where you earn money within the first year.

You build your foundation the first year. The second year, your business can generate an overflow. And the third and fourth years, many

1

entrepreneurs hit the seven-figure mark. Traditionally, that is not the case. However, with online marketing and social media, and a change of habits and belief system, you can have a business that makes vast amounts of money in two years. It can also be set up in such a way that you will have the freedom to spend time with your friends and family and have time for your fitness. We will discuss this in later chapters.

I used to be a great starter but not a good finisher. I would have great ideas, and I could speak and enroll people in my ideas, but I never followed anything through to ultimate success and freedom.

By age 39, I had been in a few different industries where I built a healthy corporate position but felt unhappy. I was unhappy because I hit certain walls. I worked for people who did not have the good habits I discovered later. So, I was under the assumption that I had to sacrifice the things that I love to stay on top.

I would exercise a couple of times a week, but I was inconsistent, so my weight would fluctuate. That too made me unhappy and caused me to lose my confidence. When I went out with my friends at dinnertime, the only thing I would have time for was a glass of wine. I also felt horrible because I never had time to take vacations.

At one point, I ran a nightclub in Las Vegas. I am a morning person, yet I sacrificed my natural rhythm to work all night long because I thought that was what it took to succeed.

Then I moved on to real estate; I ended up working six or seven days a week. Every single month for a year, I traveled to London from Las Vegas. I worked myself into the ground, and I ended up with anxiety attacks and on Xanax.

I knew there had to be a better way of achieving a successful career. Therefore, I set out on a quest to learn about personal leadership and gain happiness. I ended up quitting my job as vice president of investor relation in real estate, and I started a coaching company. I did not know what I was going to do, which proves that you do not have to know what you will do in business to make money in your first year. You only have to follow the proper formula.

I realized that you do not have to sacrifice the things that mean the most to you. You do not have to live a life without meaning to be financially independent, at peace about your retirement later in life, and able to live where you would like to. You can have time to do the things that lift you up. You can have time for a family. You can do all this, if you do things differently and stop following the old traditional model of working yourself into the ground to be successful.

Many entrepreneurs sacrifice too much to be successful. That is how the bad reputation of being an entrepreneur and making a lot of money has come about. So many people think making money is connected to giving up a lot. You do sacrifice, but there is a good sacrifice, a right sacrifice, and there is an absolute, non-negotiable sacrifice.

In this book, I will prove that it is possible to be successful while having time for the things you love. I will not just present theories; I will show you how to do it.

Perhaps you work for a corporation and know that you would love to own your company, but you do not know where to start or how to do it. This book will solve that problem for you.

Or maybe you already are an entrepreneur, and you have never made more than a $100,000 a year, or you work too much and have not taken a vacation in a long time. This book is for you.

After having read this book, you can expect to know how to build a business in two years. This business will not only pay great money and make a difference in the world, but it will also allow you time to enjoy your life. I will show you how to prioritize and schedule in a way where you work three weeks per month versus four weeks and still move your company to be worth multimillion dollars.

◆

CHAPTER 1

THE RIGHT SACRIFICES

The first thing you need to do is choose your vision. What is important to you in the life that you want to create along with the business that you want to build?

The first question I like to ask anybody who is interested in starting a business is, "How much money would you like to earn each month?" Not each year, each month. I also ask them the following questions.

- What do you want your life to look like if it could look any way you want?
- What would your work schedule look like?
- What time would you stop working?
- What would you do with your free time?
- How would your relationship with your spouse or your partner look?
- How would your body look?
- What would your hobbies be?

Build into your business what you want to make each month and what you want your life to look like because the two of them fuel each other.

When you build a business without taking into consideration the life that you want to live, you will easily burn out or get sick. You might end up with a heart attack or anxiety. You might get in a car accident because you are too tired. Something will break, if you do not learn the art of balancing your work and your lifestyle.

There are many studies about what makes people happy. First, researchers have found that any income exceeding $50,000 a year does not impact a person's happiness. Striving for more money will not necessarily give you a better life, unless you put the same emphasis on building your life as you do on building your financial freedom.

A good friend of mine who works in New York City has a job he loves. He also has a beautiful wife and two young daughters. However, he spends 50 hours a week in the office and another 10 hours a week just reading. In other words, he spends 60 hours each week in his work environment. In addition, he travels one to five nights a few times each month, which takes away more time with his family. He has been working like this for more years than I can count. He uses the excuse of, "I love my business, and I love what I do for a living." But in my opinion, he sacrifices too much. I do not believe that anybody on their deathbed says, "I wish I would have worked more."

There is another way to build financial freedom where you can enjoy life at the same time. There is a way to not sacrifice the time with your family and other things that are important to you for you to have the life and lifestyle that you want.

I have been able to build my company in less than five years. I knew nothing about the business coaching industry before then. I had worked in the nightclub industry as a general manager. I went to the University of Nevada, Las Vegas, where I studied business management with a hotel casino emphasis. I never graduated because I quickly started earning a lot of money, so I dropped out of school and followed my entrepreneurial spirit instead.

I had also worked in real estate. There I became a vice president within a year and built a division that was purely out of my mind. I had zero experience with it, so I built a team of people around me to make it happen.

Eventually, I left both industries and started my own company. Three-and-a-half years later, my company hit the seven-figure mark. How do you do that in an industry that you do not know anything about? It is easy.

Many people work their life away for the sake of trying to make money. But it is not necessary to do that. There is a new and fresh way to make money by using the Internet, building an audience, and knowing how to convert and sell. I will share with you how to do that as we move through these chapters. What I want you to take away from this chapter is that you need to develop the skill of thinking differently.

Be Willing to Take Risks

My friend who I mentioned earlier, who works 60 hours a week in New York City, is a financial broker for a huge brokers institution. He is charismatic and a great speaker. He frequently speaks at conferences, and he runs his own team. Many of his skills transfer to the entrepreneurial world. If he were to become an entrepreneur, for example, a speaker, he would no longer need to work 60 hours per week, not even in the startup phase.

To be successful in corporate America or as an entrepreneur, you have to be willing to take risks. If you are already successful in the corporate world, it is easy to also be a successful entrepreneur.

My New York friend could become a speaker and a financial coach. He could earn as much money as he wanted and keep the money in his pocket. He could be in charge of his time too.

In my company, we work with clients three days a week. The other two days of the week, we work on the marketing, research, blogging, and strategy. My schedule is set up in such a way that nobody tells me I have to take a call or run the business according to someone else's expectations. I can run it according to mine.

You have to break free from your old ways of thinking. I have seen real estate agents, salespeople, and entrepreneurs think they have to fit into the sale. They think they have to respond right away when somebody voices a need for them. However, the opposite is true. If you communicate to people the hours you are available and let them know that you are fully committed on other days of the week, you will start to train them how to treat you. You must stay consistent, which means that you cannot break your new pattern. You have to voice your pattern often when you work with people and when you are in the office.

Eventually, they start to get conditioned to when you are available, and they start fitting into your agenda versus you fitting into theirs. As you can see, this can set you up so that you never again take calls at seven or eight o'clock at night. And you will no longer work on weekends, when you might be at church, out exercising, or spending time with someone you love.

You must communicate, and you must stay consistent with that communication. Stay committed to your new schedule. If you stop trying to fit into the sale, you will quickly grow financially.

When I am overwhelmed, I think to myself that television personality Martha Stewart is running a bigger company that I am. Arianna Huffington, syndicated columnist, has more things on her to-do list than I do. And Richard Branson, founder of the Virgin Group, owns more companies than I can count, and he is not the one who does everything. These people did not become successful because they were always available for every single client and at every person's beck and call. They learned how to think and strategize differently. And that is what I am asking you to do.

I am asking you to move beyond the idea that you have to handle business the old way to be successful. To break the chain of working too hard for too little money, you will have to change the way you think, strategize, and prioritize.

THREE-MONTH TIMELINES

Every time you work on a project or an idea that you want to develop, think in three-month timelines. For instance, when we sell a coaching program, we sell it for three months. When we build a new corporate division, we divide it into three-month goals. You want to work in pushes. Human beings can push and still balance life alongside work for about three months before needing a break.

After each three-month push, you take a few days' break from work. In the three months prior, you might work extremely hard. You might ask your family, your friends, and the people around you to be considerate and let you work hard for those three months. That is your right to be dedicated to your work. After those three months, you need to disconnect.

Educator and businessman Stephen Covey talks about habits of successful people. According to Covey, you want to think in small milestones.

We have a division called HeartCore Endurance, where we train entrepreneurs to train for half marathons and marathons. Business professionals often neglect their health and HeartCore Endurance solves that problem for them.

When we birthed the program, we had a three-month timeline of selling the program to a small group of people. Instead of striving for my ultimate vision of having 2,000 people in the program, we went with a three-month goal of having 20 people in it. Selling the program to 20 people in three months was a stretch. We had to figure out our message, our marketing strategy, and how to find 60 people to close 20. Even if it was a stretch, it was attainable, and it earned the company $111,000 in 90 days.

I might have been able to reach the three-month goal we set only by working during regular business hours, or I might have hit a wall and would need to work a couple of late nights during the three-month period. Because it was for a limited period, I had the energy to do it.

The three-month end date is helpful to those around you. After three months, you take time off work, and you take the family on a weekend trip or something relaxing. You turn off your phone and your computer, and you inform everybody that you will be with your family for the next four days.

After your time away, for the next 30 or 60 days, you work normal hours and have dinner with the family. Then you pick up another three-month tempo when you strive toward another goal. Too many goals in a year will burn you out.

Who cares if you make a million dollars this year or if you make a million dollars next year, and it takes you a year longer to get to your destination? If you did not enjoy the process, it was a failure.

If you push for more than three months, you run the risk of becoming sloppy. When you become sloppy, you get tired, and then you make mistakes that cost you money. The worst thing an entrepreneur can ever do is be too busy. If you are too busy, you are not intimate enough with the projects that are on your plate. If you are not intimate with the projects on your plate, you will lose money through the cracks. You will start feeling overwhelmed. Now and then, you might have a hard time catching your breath. You work too fast and too hard, and you make mistakes. You do not have the time to read documents or think of ideas or brainstorm in a way that puts you ahead.

If you communicate and stay consistent and committed, it helps create the structure around your three-month timeline or your three-month tempo. During the three months, you run a short race, and you run wholeheartedly. The three-month tempo creates structure that prevents you from falling apart.

COMMIT TO THE NEW STRUCTURE

An entrepreneur might say, "Okay, I will only work three days a week on this project, and I will have meetings for this project on Monday, Tuesday, and Wednesday." Then somebody phones and requests an important meeting for Saturday. If you agree, your whole structure is torn down.

You must commit to your structure and live in abundance versus scarcity. I have only lost one client my entire life as a consequence of not compromising on my structure. I take off the month of December, and one client just would not wait another month. I lost that one $35,000 client and, let me be honest, there was another client right behind that person.

You might think that you always have to be available for clients or that you must be in the office on Saturday. You might think that you have to fly to another city, even though your child has an important soccer game. You might believe that these are the sacrifices you must make to earn money. But that is not true.

If entrepreneurs never commit to their schedules, they will always chase the money. What happens when you chase anything? It runs from you. It is a universal law. You have to break that pattern. You have to think differently.

Most people think they have to take whatever is coming their way and sacrifice whatever it takes to reach their goals. However, that is not what successful people do—not those who have a life of wellness, fitness, great relationships, and a great income. Many people are successful while sacrificing too much. Those individuals typically end up in a hospital bed later in life.

I love my stepfather, Don. One of the things that I love is what he did when he made his first $25,000—his first large sum of money. His family and friends told him that he should meet with a financial advisor and invest in a 401(k) and secure his retirement.

However, Don went out and bought his first boat. Everybody thought he was insane because he bought a boat that was fancy and big for the time, many years ago. He invested in the boat so that he could detach from work. He loved being on it. Every time he drove his boat, he solved the problems in his business. Happiness opens the mind for creativity!

Don went against the grain, which is what many successful people do to become successful. Spending time on his boat allowed him to relax.

When we relax, we open up. We are sometimes too close to a problem to solve it. It is often easy to see the solution for somebody else's problem because you are not inside it. You need to move outside your problems to grow your life and your business. What allows you to do that is having a life.

Don now boats around the world. He is always set up for entertaining because he has friends and family around him all the time. He said to me on our last boat trip, "I have never gotten on my boat and not solved a problem in my business. Whenever I need to figure something out, I get on the boat and just go."

I share that story with you because I want you to realize that this is a strategy and permission for you to stop sacrificing the important things in your life. By prioritizing the things that make you happy, you create space in your mind and your heart. Then you will see how to make money and find solutions to problems that you have been trying to solve for years. Your challenge is to let go of old habits and beliefs and to think differently.

◆

CHAPTER 2

CONTROLLERS, PERFECTIONISTS, AND PROCRASTINATORS

L isten up, because this chapter can help you.

Success thrives on uncertainty. It also thrives on your ability to move beyond this feeling and become comfortable with uncertainty.

As human beings, we constantly try to build our businesses, cash flow, and freedom, based on what we are most comfortable with.

I teach strategies to entrepreneurs. For instance, I can teach them a three-step process for building their audience. After they have learned the strategy, they will want to rinse and repeat, because now it has become a part of their comfort zone. However, during the learning process, they must become comfortable with the energy and mental state of uncertainty. It is critical for them to be able to move forward with any new project.

Most people want to put together a fully thought-out plan. That is fine at certain stages of building a business, but if you have not yet reached financial freedom, you need to develop the muscle of uncertainty first.

Every step-by-step plan I have worked on has changed in the buildout, and without mental strength to stay on track, things fall apart quickly!

When a new year starts, you might map out a plan for your goals and how you are going to reach them. At the beginning of the year, you feel inspired. However, as the year goes by, most people do not complete what they set out to do, or they only complete a portion of it. They let family, time, travel, death, or something get in the way. It prevents them from executing their plan, and they settle for that.

HOW TO OVERCOME CHALLENGES

If you want to be wildly successful and have the freedom that gives you the flexibility to handle challenges that come up, you have to excel at rolling with the punches. Life will keep throwing you death. Life will keep throwing you taxes. Life will keep challenging you with maintenance on your house. If you use those reasons to stop or procrastinate executing your plan, you will never achieve great success because those things will never stop coming.

Whenever I am faced with a challenge, I think that God gave me that challenge to strengthen me, so I can improve the skill to handle whatever comes my way.

The backward thought we often think is that challenges are fate or reasons to quit. Or we think that they are so big that what we are doing might not be right, and we give up. That is a faulty mindset.

If you could become great at identifying the moments when you want to stop because you are afraid, because you do not know the full plan, or because you are not clear about what you will sell, you will become a much better entrepreneur. Then you can roll with the moments of uncertainty that will come, and you will get to your goal.

At HeartCore Business, we have a program called the Profit Acceleration Club for Entrepreneurs or PACE. In this club, we usually have between 130 and 150 business owners from around the world. Some of them have been in business for five or six years, without their annual income exceeding six or seven figures. And about 40 percent of the people who enroll do not even know what they will sell or what their business is going to be. What they do have is a *core calling of having freedom in their life*. It does not matter whether or not they know what they will do. At some point in developing any project, there will be uncertainty, so becoming comfortable with it is critical.

When we take the members of PACE through a yearlong program, we do not tell them what the next step is, and we omit this information on purpose. We leave it out because we want them to become comfortable without knowing what is coming. We want to strengthen that muscle, so they can let go of their perfectionism and their need to control and know what is ahead.

The sister of perfectionism is procrastination. By learning to become comfortable with uncertainty, the perfectionism and procrastination that has stopped many entrepreneurs goes away.

The first 90 days of the PACE program, we teach our members how to build a list—an audience. Afterward, we teach them how to survey that audience so that they can know what their audience wants. Then we create a product that we market. That is how you create a product whether you are an author, a business coach, a financial advisor, or a real estate agent. By following this process, we will know what the marketplace wants, and then we can create a product that sells easily.

To download a sample of a survey, go to **http://www.heartcorebusiness.com/survey**.

PACE has a 94 percent success rate. Our high success rate is because we teach the members how to let go of the rookie mentality of needing to know every step to the end. We only give them one step to work on at a time, which is the key to master uncertainty. We show them how to think like an entrepreneur. They all want to know what comes next and what they are going to sell. They get ahead of themselves. All they need to know in the beginning is what they want, how much money they want to make per month, and what they want their schedule to look like. Once they have determined that, we will build the plan to get there. It does not matter what they are going to sell before they have clients. For that reason, we work on building the client list or the audience first.

If you begin a project and then run into a brick wall, it tests your commitment to the project. *Entrepreneurs need to follow a project all the way through to their goals; they must always hit their numbers.*

Nicole is one of our clients, and she has been with us for three years. She was originally a love coach. The first year she went to PACE, she built a list, and we taught her how to sell to that list. Like many entrepreneurs, Nicole ran into brick walls after starting her project. She felt it was difficult and did not know if she wanted to do it anymore. She thought that relationships were not her core calling.

However, I would not let her give up, because you cannot quit halfway through a plan in our HeartCore Business model. That is a bad habit that entrepreneurs have, and the worst thing that can happen to entrepreneurs is that they lose their confidence. Many start without much confidence because they have never done this before.

A friend of mine, Robyn Benincasa, wrote a book called *How Winning Works.* In this book, she states, "Commitment starts when the fun stops." Nicole had some logical reasons for giving up on her business. One of the biggest reasons was that she did not feel passionate about it anymore. Usually, nobody will fight you when you feel that way.

A professional operates based on commitment. An amateur operates based on feelings. You have to manage yourself and be professional, or else you will never achieve financial freedom.

Nicole struggled through her uncertainty and experiences of people hanging up on her when she spoke to them on the phone. She had a brutal sales campaign to sell out her first private program as a love coach. However, she stuck to it, and she developed grit—mental strength.

Today, Nicole teaches women around the world how to own their sexuality, how to own their self-love, and how to walk into any room and attract the right man. In other words, she teaches people how to flirt. There are many people who would love to know how to walk into a room and get attention, and Nicole does that. Her business would never have opened up and flourished into what it was meant to be if she had given up in the beginning. Then she could not see what was around the corner. Around the corner was a heart-centered, fulfilling core calling that her soul, God, or whatever you want to call it, was trying to get her to. She now has a full practice. In her second year in business, she earned $160,000.

When most people are inspired, they never get the idea off the paper. Nicole's story proves to me and should also prove to you that creating the plan is not the most important step. What is most important is to take the plan from the start all the way to finish.

You should be able to admit what you want and do whatever it takes to get there. You might be ashamed to admit that you want to be a millionaire if you only make $40,000 a year. However, you have to be able to state what you want unashamedly to your friends and people around you. Saying your goal to those around you is what brings you into alignment with it. It makes you accountable and committed to it. As you admit it and do whatever it takes to get it, you begin to work through some of the self-doubt and embarrassment.

Many dreams are smothered from logical reasoning to wait. I invite you to stop it right now.

◆◆◆

CHAPTER 3

THE FREEDOM MODEL

People tend to listen to advice from the wrong people. When I wanted to fall in love, I did not listen to my friends who had average marriages. I hired a relationship coach who works with professional women who tend to be busy and have a type A personality. I got advice specifically from somebody who understood who I was, and I am her ideal client.

All too often, entrepreneurs take advice from their friends and family who are not entrepreneurs, or they take advice from peers who have yet to be wildly prosperous.

Doing whatever it takes means positioning yourself so that you can learn from those who have been successful. It could be hiring a good coach, interning at a company, or working for somebody who has made great achievements. By seeking the influence of successful people and listening to their advice exclusively, you can imitate their results.

STOP MAKING EXCUSES

The next thing you need to do is give up the idea of your body breaking down. People hold back far too often. Do not let sickness, body aches, or something along those lines hold you back. It rains on successful people, and it rains on unsuccessful people. That is never going to end.

I have clients who have built their list (or audience) from a hospital bed while undergoing chemotherapy. They have testified to us that developing their business was the purpose that helped them focus on something healing and fulfilling, instead of surrendering to the pain or breaking down.

I also have clients who like to hide behind God or the fact that their body is telling them to quit. God put the dream of building a business in your heart and head in the first place. Go all the way. Then tell me how you feel!

As I go through this chapter, you will see that I am all about having freedom of time and taking care of yourself. However, most of the people I coach hold back because of limited thought patterns disguised as reasons.

My business coach serves as a great example of the opposite. One time, as she was hosting an event with 700 people, she had a heart problem and was rushed to the emergency room. There, a doctor stuck a needle in her heart, killed her, and boosted her heart back to life. Then, with no sleep, she went back into the room with the 700 people and continued training them the next day.

Another great example is motivational speaker Les Brown. He once came off the stage and collapsed in people's arms because his cancer was extremely painful, and then he went back on stage and made a difference.

You have to learn what it takes to access freedom. Some of you might say that is not for you. Okay, then give up the dream in your heart and live peacefully with what you have. That is okay!

I was listening to televangelist Joel Osteen on the radio the other day, and he was talking about how the palm tree is considered the tree that bounces back. A hurricane can push the tree all the way down, almost to the ground for five hours or so, and the tree will bounce back with a stronger root system—much like every time you overcome a life storm.

When Osteen started his ministry, people told him he would not be a good minister. He used to come off the stage and think that he was not good enough. However, he did not allow that to stop him, and today he has a massive church. He is also on TV and has his own radio show. He has had extraordinary funding to get him to where he is today, and the floodgates of heaven have opened up for him.

I do not share this with you because of religion or faith. My point is that you will have to go through your version of a hurricane, and you have to be strong enough and develop enough grit to be able to bounce back. The hurricane could be anything ranging from the realm of faith, to money, to health, to love, to business.

If you submit to excuses every time an obstacle occurs, you will not make it. What I ask of you is to stop telling other people who have a dream in their heart to hold back. Just because you hold back does not mean that you should influence other people to do the same.

Be people's best cheerleader. We already know that we get further if we work in teams. When I listen to entrepreneurs and most networking groups and mastermind groups, I hear people aid others' excuses to hold back. You must stop listening to such talk. Instead, start learning how to overcome those challenges.

The skill that you need to develop is how to stay committed to your goal despite hurdles.

DEVELOP GRIT

As mentioned previously, we have a program in HeartCore Business called HeartCore Endurance. In this program, we teach entrepreneurs around the world, virtually over conference lines, how to develop grit. How we do this is to train them for half marathons. It is not running the race that is hard. The challenge is sticking to the training plan while you have kids, life, family, an injury, and a business to take care of at the same time. The more challenging the physical training curriculum for training for the half marathon is, the more challenging that plan is. It is different to prepare for a marathon in a community than alone with a trainer. In our community, everybody is an entrepreneur, so they have a clear picture of what they want to accomplish. The preparation for the half marathon improves their capacity to grow more and hold more tasks in their company.

Whenever I feel overwhelmed, I think about others who have a much bigger business and more children than I have. I think about how they deal with more obstacles than I do and still happily run the race. That gives me perspective on my thoughts of not being able to handle a situation because I have not done it before, or it is out of my comfort zone. The key is to make your goal the new normal.

If you have a hard time developing grit, look up HeartCore Business and the HeartCore Endurance program. Join us, because there is no way you will achieve your goal by meditation or pure willpower.

I used to be an excellent starter and a horrible finisher. It was through training for races that I became mentally and strategically stronger and more capable of following a plan to the end. No course, miracle, motivational book, or CD could get me to do what it took to be successful. Training for a race was what did it.

THE DIFFERENT STAGES OF THE FREEDOM MODEL

There are many different models of building a business that work. There is a model that works and gives you time freedom, money freedom, and hobby freedom, so that you can live your life. It's the Freedom Model.

FREEDOM MODEL

LIST BUILD

HIGH END   MID   LOW END

SKILL: MASTER SALES

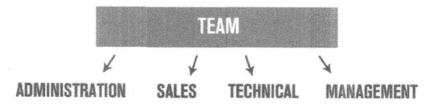

TEAM

ADMINISTRATION   SALES   TECHNICAL   MANAGEMENT

SKILL: LEADERSHIP - WHO ARE YOUR "LIFER" EMPLOYEES?

GET KNOWN

YOU CEO

REPLACE YOURSELF   OPERATIONS   HUMAN RESOURCES

SKILL: SELLING WITHOUT YOU; DOING FULFILLMENT 401K, HEALTH INSURANCE, LIFELONG

BIGGER VISION

The reason you Became an Entrepreneur in the First Place
TIME TO BECOME THE FACE PERSON OF YOUR COMPANY

LIST BUILD

On the top of the flowchart is priority number one, which is to build a list. The list is your audience. In Chapter 5, I will show you how to build your list.

You need to own your list. On free social media platforms, such as Facebook, Instagram, and LinkedIn, they can sell or move your data at any time because you do not own the platform—you do not pay for it. Considering all the money you spend on building your list, you certainly want to own it. We use Infusionsoft to collect names, phone numbers, addresses, and so on. However, I started on AWeber. It is an inexpensive place to keep your list.

It does not matter what you will sell at this point. What matters is what you care about and what your field or industry is. Then you build a list on that topic.

After creating the list, you need to begin selling three things: a high-end product, a midrange product, and a low-end product. As a CEO, the skill that you need to master at this point is sales. *The next step after this will be team building.*

TEAM

Many entrepreneurs want to jump to first creating a team because they think their life is busy and they need more people to support and help them, but they do not.

Your first focus should be to sell your high-end product, because that is what brings in the most money with the least amount of sales. The midrange product is what makes you wealthy. The low-end product takes a lot longer to build. Most entrepreneurs want to start with the low-end product because they think it is the least risky, but I want you to start on the high end.

Once you have mastered the sales of these products, you move on to building your team. The first person you need to employ is an admin. There is virtual assistance around the world who can help you. They are not expensive, because you usually will not require them to work 40 hours per week, and they can work from anywhere, so you do not necessarily need an office to house them.

I know people who earn $5 million a year and are entirely virtual. At HireMyMom.com, you can find great writers, admins, and other professionals. You can also post an advertisement and interview people.

If you want to run any virtual business or attract customers online, you need a tech team. Your tech team could be just one person who helps you put up online pages, advertisements, etc. To limit your number of staff, you can hire an admin who knows how to do that. The subject line for that job description could be, "Savvy, technical, virtual assistant needed."

The next step is hiring a salesperson. Your salesperson is critical to the success of your business. The best salespeople are typically those you have trained or worked with, or someone who has been your raving client or customer for a year. You can give them leads and pay them a good percentage, for example, 20 percent of what they sell.

The fourth and last person you need to hire is a management team, and that might just be one person. If you build your company the way that I suggest, then, within a couple of years, you will have more business than you can handle. That is when you hit the breaking point as the CEO, and you need to take off a hat. When you take that hat off, you usually put it on a manager to help project manage your company.

The CEO skill that you need to develop for building a team is leadership. I recommend the book *The One Minute Manager*, by management expert/physician Ken Blanchard and thought leader/physician Spencer Johnson, to anybody who finds it difficult to manage their time or lead people, or repeatedly experiences that their employees quit. This book will teach you how to stop doing other people's jobs and start empowering those around you to be successful.

GET KNOWN

The third step in the flowchart is what entrepreneurs commonly want to do as their first step, which is to become known in their industry. A long time ago, I was taught, "grow slow, fire fast." The Freedom Model would make most entrepreneurs feel like they are growing fast because they have results within two years, and their business is growing consistently.

You do not want to become known until you have done the following: You have built your list. You have sold a high-end, a midrange, and a low-end product. And you have at least developed your admin team, tech team, and sales team. Can you imagine if, all of a sudden, you were on the *Today* TV show and you were not set up for the inflow that would come because you did not have a team and existing community that you have sold to? You would not be prepared for success, and success loves preparation.

P.S. You can easily earn millions of dollars a year and still not be known.

Once you have completed the first two steps, you are ready to become known. How do you become an influencer in your field? That funnels into you becoming the true CEO of your company. The CEO's primary responsibility is to drive a vision. Up until now, you have been doing a lot of the grunt work yourself. At this point, you are probably moving into the third year of your business, and it is time to consider replacing yourself.

It is time to start thinking about the operation, and it is time to start thinking about a human resource (HR) department, which could be one person. You can make millions of dollars with just a couple of people in each department.

When you become the true CEO, you look for people in your organization who can replace you. You look for somebody to bring on at a significant pay rate to do operations for your company, so that you can take off another major hat. Even if your company only consists of three or four people, you now want somebody to move into HR so that he or she can make sure that your team is happy.

Happy people perform better. Money is not a motivator; they have to feel appreciated. As a small business owner, you have many great opportunities to make your employees happy. For instance, my staff have the following benefits.

- They can work part-time at home and part-time in the office.
- They receive two weeks paid vacation.
- They have opportunities to be on our sales team to bump their incomes higher than what their pay rate would ever be in the normal economic marketplace.
- We give them lavish bonuses.
- We send gifts to their families.
- We treat them and their spouses to date nights at exclusive restaurants.
- We send them thank-you cards, throughout the year, thanking them for specific things they have done for the company.

Your HR person can help you find out what makes each of your employees feel appreciated, so you are not guessing. The job of the HR person is to make sure you are staying in compliance with your employees and also make sure that your employees are happy.

When you step into the role of the CEO of your business, you must learn to let go of control in different areas of how your company is run. Instead, empower the right people.

Someone like Richard Branson is not controlling every single move in all his companies. He cannot do that and be as successful as he has been. So why do you think you can?

It is wonderful when you evolve to the final and last stage in the Freedom Model, which is what you are made to do. Now that your company operates well, all the way from building your list to being the CEO and pushing the vision of your company, you get to do whatever you want to do. Your life is now funded.

At this stage, you can ask yourself, "What do I most feel like doing today?" You have the money and the time available, because you have built a great team, and you have the space to be creative. This is how the Freedom Model works.

What typically happens in the normal way of building a business is you have an idea, you map out every step of that idea, and it never gets off the ground. You run the rat race, work 60 hours a week, and your health declines. Eventually, you might end up with broken relationships and a critical disease because stress can kill you. Once that happens to you, then you say that making money is hard, and you repeat that message to all those who have a dream to do it differently than you, and you crush their dreams.

The good news is there is a better way to build your business. The Freedom Model is the fresh approach that will give you everything you look for. If you want to get started now or talk to a business coach, please reach out to us on our website. On the "Let's Talk" pop-up box on the HeartCore Business blog, you can type in your business question and have a business coach reach out to you free of charge and discuss your plan for success with you. Lock in your vision, and let's see what you are made of.

◆◆◆

CHAPTER 4

LEARN HOW TO PRIORITIZE

The reason entrepreneurs around the world hire me has a lot to do with my lifestyle. My lifestyle largely comes down to how I prioritize my time. Even though my company grows by 30 percent each year, I am still living a life outside work. If you have built your business correctly by following the Freedom Model that we talked about in the previous chapter, you should have more free time as your business expands.

As we discussed, when you work on a big project, you should spend 90 days turning up the heat, working long hours, and working hard to get the project done. However, you cannot keep up that tempo indefinitely without burning out.

FLEXTIME

If you have a meeting to go to that takes place an hour away, and you leave exactly an hour open to get there, you do not have enough flextime to correct your course if something goes wrong. There could be an accident on the way, or your car could stall.

We have all seen people come late to meetings for different reasons. Things happen, and we understand that. But what is interesting is that things happen to the same people repeatedly.

You want to risk manage your business and your life. That way, when things go wrong (because they will), you have enough room to solve the problem and remain committed to whatever you said you would do.

How does this work in business? First, you have to create a schedule that allows you to be smart. All brilliant people have time and space to be quiet. It helps them see the solutions to the problems that they try to solve.

Other entrepreneurs have chaotic lifestyles. They are always answering their phones, checking emails, responding to people coming into their offices, and they are in meetings back-to-back. Entrepreneurs like these might make a lot of money, but they tend to burn out. And when you analyze their profits, you see that they are not as good as you might think.

The way that you make great money while enjoying your life is by having flextime. It is the new and fresh approach to being an entrepreneur, and it is the key to success.

On the fourth week of every month, my calendar is clear. I do not meet with clients; I do not have appointments. I only schedule time with friends and time to take care of me and those around me. It leaves me seven consecutive days to pay extra attention to my son, go to the spa, or do something else that makes me feel fulfilled and happy.

The other day, one of my clients asked, "How do you stick to your flextime?" I told her, "It's non-negotiable." She has watched me for a couple of years and has seen my company continue to grow without my calendar and my ability to stay present with people depleting. I have been consistent in who I am, though the company has grown.

My secret to remaining who I am is not allowing myself to be overwhelmed. I might have moments where I feel like I just have to get something done, but I do not feel overwhelmed on a consistent basis. I am not driving my nervous system into a brick wall. That allows me to be present with people and easily solve problems.

I also take off the month of December. It takes me about two weeks before my brain stops thinking about business, and I unwind. The first two weeks when I stop working and have that flextime, I solve problems. I will have aha moments while walking down the street. It happens because when you open up and let go of the busy energy, you get smarter. Fight-or-flight energy shuts down your brain and prevents you from thinking.

If you cannot give yourself space or flextime, chances are you will solve problems in your company with an okay decision, not with an extraordinary decision that moves your company in quantum leaps. The old saying is that the person who is the most successful is the person who solves the most problems. The person who procrastinates is caught up in perfectionism. Because of perfectionism, that person has a hard time making a decision. Then she or he stalls and is always left behind. In other words, it is not necessarily the most talented who make it to the top.

It is difficult to make good decisions when you do not give yourself enough space. You must disconnect from technology, your office, your emails, your staff—all that. Then you must go do something fun. Something fun might be having a movie marathon on Netflix for a couple of days, or it could be going on a three-day hike in the Grand Canyon. It all depends on who you are. The important thing is to get out and live a life you enjoy on a consistent basis. When you enjoy life, you will make more money.

In regard to your business, first you need to choose the ideal rhythm that works for you. Some people might not like the idea of taking a whole week off every month.

When I started this rhythm, I needed to break my workaholism, because I was working all the time. Even though I made a lot of money for the corporation that I worked for, I never made a ton of money myself. That had to do with the fact that I could never get outside my work to negotiate the best deal possible for myself. Paradoxically, I did not have enough time to work on my business because I was investing so much time in my business. I did not believe that I could take a whole week off.

You too might be in a situation where you cannot see how taking a whole week off is possible. If that is the case, then we need to enhance your problem-solving skills, because it is possible.

Richard Branson, Martha Stewart, and others like them have more on their plates than the majority of entrepreneurs who are reading this book. However, they find ways to take vacations and follow their passions. They enjoy space and time. And most deals are made during fun times. Most people know this conceptually, but they do not apply it because they think that is the life they get when they are successful. But it is the other way around; you get that successful life when you start operating like this.

Choose the rhythm that works best for you. When I first started implementing flextime, I decreased my workweek to three days, and I became depressed. You might ask yourself, "Shanda, why are you trying to set me up with a schedule that might make me depressed?" The reason I shared this with you is because when you start to make your life about more than work, you might not know what to do with it. You might not know what to do with your time. Unless you are busy chasing the mighty dollar or some level of success or power, you might feel unproductive. Perhaps you do not like sitting by yourself, and maybe nobody is around to spend time with you.

THE RESULTS

What happens when you start to take time off work is you begin to get intimate with yourself. It is important because intimacy is how you make good decisions. Intimacy is how you move a project forward. If you are to become intimate with a project, you have to slow down enough to spend time with it.

Intimacy does not mean spending five hours one day working on a project while also taking 16 phone calls and going to three meetings. If you do that, you might end up only dedicating an hour and a half to the project. You have to create that intimacy and space to be able to be successful.

Flextime enhances your power and skills in running your business. Consider what rhythm would be ideal for you. For instance, Fridays might be good days for you to work half days or take off. Start whittling down the time that you spend in the office, empowering somebody else to get the job done. Otherwise, you can't start doing less because you still have commitments. So, start practicing doing less and letting go of control gradually, while still getting the job done. Here is where you heighten and sharpen your problem-solving skills.

If you practice what I am talking about, your flextime will continue to grow. I started with a three-day workweek, dealt with my depression issues, and began enjoying life outside work. Now, I have found the rhythm that suits me where I work three weeks per month and then take one week off. The seven days off in a row helps me enjoy my life and not become overwhelmed.

If you pay attention during the next week, you will see when you work best. Perhaps you are focused in the morning but lose focus after three o'clock in the afternoon. If so, maybe you can stop working at 3:00 p.m. on Thursdays and Fridays.

I promise you that your flextime will grow—and grow quickly—if you stay committed to it. I like to train for triathlons, so I make that a priority. Because when I am happy, I make better decisions, I am more energetic and enthusiastic at work, and I make more money. I work from 9:00 a.m. until my last appointment at 3:00 p.m. I am usually done anywhere between 3:30 and 4:00 p.m. I like to be out of the office by 4:00. That allows me to go train for triathlons, go running, go biking, and whatever else I want to do in the evenings. I swim for triathlons in the mornings. I always take off on Saturday and Sunday. I only work with clients on Monday, Tuesday, and Wednesday, which allows me to work on my business on Thursday and Friday.

This schedule is non-negotiable. I do not reschedule appointments with clients to Thursday and Friday, even if they have a scheduling conflict. I let them know that I do apologize, but the days I work with clients are Monday, Tuesday, and Wednesday mornings. This rhythm allows me two-and-a-half days a week to do online marketing, work with my team, think about other projects, mind map, write books, and whatever else I need and want to do. It allows me the time to work on other projects that inspire me and help me move my company forward.

For all those who are parents, being done at work by 4:00 p.m., not working weekends, taking a week off work each month, and making millions of dollars—that is freedom.

As I mentioned before, I also take the month of December off, and that is my family time. I go skiing, visit my parents in Canada, and spend quality time with my family. I, like most entrepreneurs, work harder than many others but being able to take a whole month off to spend with family is wonderful.

HOW TO MAKE FLEXTIME IN YOUR LIFE

The first step toward achieving this life is to choose your ideal rhythm and stick to it. Design it with your life in mind first and then fit productivity around that.

The second step is communicating your business schedule with your family, your peers, your clients, and your staff, virtual assistants, or whoever works with you. It is important to communicate it with them, not just once but constantly. I advocate flextime every time I speak onstage, during virtual training online, in this book, and with my friends. I speak about it constantly so that no one is confused why they cannot reach me.

Once, on the fourth week of the month, one of my clients sent me the following text message: "I so apologize, I know it's your flex week, but I have this urgent thing coming up." I might receive a text message like that in a flex week. But, for the most part, my clients wait until I am back in the office. That is created and not by accident.

Clients will manage their lives and their schedules because they know I am not available then. This is why it is critical to communicate your schedule and do so repeatedly in conversation with people. Tell them what you do and why. What is amazing is they will start to respect you for operating this way, and, believe it or not, many of them will adopt the formula.

The third step is to guard your schedule and stay committed to it no matter what. Many of my clients who incorporate flextime into their schedule mirror my rhythm and take a week off each month. One of my clients, a chiropractor, does just that. I first met her when I spoke at a live event in San Diego. She hid in the bathroom because her business was so busy that she did not want to be in the networking break. She did not want to meet anybody who needed a chiropractor.

Talk about hiding from your business. She is a mother, she was overworked, and she was not enjoying being an entrepreneur. Due to all the stress, she was debating closing her business.

One thing that I focus on when I teach entrepreneurs is how to make a business virtual. When the chiropractor became my client, we even created a virtual business for her. It has given her time freedom and money freedom. She still has her brick-and-mortar business, but she runs it differently with flextime. And now she loves her business.

She makes more money than before, and she is passionate about what she does. Less than a year ago, she wanted to close it, but now she aspires to continue growing it.

You have to guard your schedule, even if you think that you have to take a certain deal or phone call. Maintain your integrity. In marketing, this is a well-established principle. When you start marketing a sale, you must stick to your parameters with the three-day sale. If you always bend it and instead make it a four-day sale, you teach your audience that you do not mean what you say. Then they will not believe you and will have no urgency. You have to stay consistent. You hurt yourself, and you hurt the way other people treat you when you bend your rule. Stick to your schedule and stay committed to it no matter what.

What if a big deal comes up, a chance in a lifetime—do you bend your flextime? This is my answer every time: The more successful you become, the more opportunities come on your plate.

I could be working 7 days a week, 365 days a year. I receive one or two offers each week to speak somewhere, do some amazing joint venture partnership, etcetera. If it is a great opportunity, I acknowledge that and look at it. Remember, the purpose of flextime is to make you a better problem solver, give you space to make better decisions, and keep your well-being up so that you are happy. Happy people make more money.

Then I check my plan. What am I working on right now? Does this project feed into that, or is it in left field but still an amazing idea or opportunity? If it is not part of what I call my ascension plan—the plan I am working on that year—I respectfully decline no matter who is involved. Do not chase the mighty dollar.

If you have a work plan, and an opportunity comes up that fits into your plan, then consider moving forward with it. That is it. Here is the deal: Confidence sells. When you are confident, you will have no shortage of opportunities to grow your plan. I have never lost a deal because of honoring my flextime. If there is something I want to do and it fits my calendar, I will not give up my flextime, but I will find another way of doing it.

◆◆◆

CHAPTER 5

BUILD YOUR AUDIENCE

The old way of building an audience is the long and hard road to becoming an entrepreneur. It is based on networking, education or certifications, or the good old word-of-mouth referrals.

The Internet has brought us a new and fresh approach. It has opened doors and avenues that allow us to build an audience much more quickly and efficiently. I saw a post on Instagram that said, "Entrepreneurship is the new retirement plan." I thought that was brilliant. Although this book is about building financial freedom within two years, you could follow the same process and retire in five years, if you do it right. Think about that for a second. In five years, you could retire or be financially set. You could have replaced yourself in your business so that you can live the life of your choice. It is possible.

My company is more than five years old. If I wanted to stop working, I could probably be out in a year, which means it would have taken me six years. But my first vision was never to retire in five years. Now that I have done it and coached many people along the way, I realize that if you are thinking about a retirement plan, the magic number ends up being five years.

In Chapter 3, we discussed the Freedom Model. The Freedom Model puts you in a position where you do not have to work forever. It will gradually make your company less dependent on you, so you will be safe financially, even if you have to attend to something in your life.

Many people have made it to the top in corporate America, but then the economy changes and people's commissions and salaries are cut in half. It is not the fault of the corporations, because they have to survive.

When you run your own ship, you decide how much you pay yourself, and you can control what happens in your economy, which is tied to your audience. And that is what we will discuss in this chapter.

In the marketing world, another word for your audience is your list. When you own a list, and you know how to take care of it, you have created your own economy. You might think, "The people on that list are subject to the economy." That is true, but remember that you have a relationship with them. You can influence them to spend their money with you, rather than online shopping or buying what they do not need.

Almost every person I know who owns a small or medium business—businesses that make anywhere between $100,000 and $5 million—usually does better when the economy breaks down. That is because they have a list and an audience who trusts them.

My favorite way to build an audience is the so-called reporter model. Barbara Walters, Oprah, and Larry King are powerful figures of our time. They follow the reporter model by speaking to other influential people or people with good stories that entertain their audiences. Consequently, viewers repeatedly tune in to their shows. You can replicate this reporter model by using the Internet and interviewing successful people. I will go into details on how to make this work later.

CHOOSE YOUR TOPIC

First, pick a topic about your interest, your product, or your service. You do not need to know what you are going to sell before you build an audience. You can build your audience before creating your product. The reason many people find it difficult to succeed is because they create their product first and then look for the audience. The truth is that doing it the other way around is easier.

One of the first audiences I built was for something called the "Feminine Shift." I built an audience of about 3,800 names and made many thousands of dollars during the next couple of months.

There is no wrong theme. I have seen people follow the reporter model to educate others about what is happening in the Middle East. I have also seen it done to change the way people date, have sex, garden, do business, and market on Facebook. The sky is the limit. It is all about what you want your theme to be.

If you do not know what you are going to sell, pick a topic that interests you. If you do know what you are going to sell, then pick an audience base or a theme that will attract your ideal clients. You build your audience the same way, whether you sell a product or coaching.

FIND YOUR EXPERTS

Once you have made your choice, you create a series of interviews. You conduct interviews about a certain topic to educate the market on a possible solution to a problem. You might do a reporter model where you interview 21 people.

You can interview more, but 21 is a magical number for building a list, consisting of between 1,700 and 2,300 people. If you, for example, are in the healthcare industry, you search online for health products and information concerning your specific topics. Look for authors who have written books about these topics.

The next thing you do is look for reviews written on Amazon about these books to gain insight on how successful the author is. One or two reviews are not enough. If the book has 20, 40, 60, or more written reviews, then I recommend that you go to the author's website and see if there is an opt-in box. An opt-in box is where the author gives away something for free to collect traffic on the Internet. You will need to give your name, email, and sometimes your phone number. An opt-in box indicates that the author has a list. But let me caution you, that it does not guarantee that they have a list.

We teach the reporter model during the course of a year in the Profit Acceleration Club for Entrepreneurs (PACE). We teach entrepreneurs how to build an audience in 90 days. It takes 90 days to do it the first time because you have never done it before. After you have done it once, it will probably take you anywhere from 30 to 45 days to do the whole process.

If I lost my list, or I moved to another country, or I decided to change industries, I know that I can make money from anywhere in the world under any topic within 45 days. Think about the freedom this gives you emotionally and financially!

So, here is the deal with the authors: You want to ask them if your subject inspires them and if they want to be a part of it. If they are positive, you invite them to be an expert and be interviewed by you for your series. Then, you will also ask them what their list size is. They need to have a list of 5,000 people or more.

Millions of people have a list of 5,000 or more. I teach this model in PACE. Many entrepreneurs tend to get stuck here. Do not give up. Entrepreneurs tend to think that there is nobody out there with a list this size. At HeartCore Business, we do the reporter model once or twice a year. That is why we have 165,000 people on our list. We average a list size of 25,000 or more to be an expert at our summits.

One of my current clients, who works in the food industry, has almost 200,000 people on his list, and he interviews big names. In other words, this works with big names and small names. Just do it!

There are many ways you can play with this to be successful. What you cannot do is interview somebody with fewer than 5,000 people on their list. The reason is that every expert will promote the event. Say the expert has a list of 5,000 names, and 20 percent (which is a good open rate) open the email that was sent to promote your free event. That means that 1,000 people opened the email.

Of those 1,000 people, not all will go to your registration page and give you their data to be a part of your free event. But let's say that 3 percent do, which is 30 people. That is on the low end. Typically, 100–200 people per expert will register for your free event. If you have 21 experts, you are looking at building a list of 2,100. We usually see entrepreneurs build their first lists to consist of 1,700–2,300 people.

CREATE THE REGISTRATION PAGE

Once you have found your experts, create your registration page, otherwise referred to as an opt-in page. This page can be a picture of you with a voice recording on autoplay or a video of you welcoming people to your free event.

It is critical that you introduce yourself and hook them into the solution that this free event is going to give them. For instance, *Oprah's Lifeclass*, a TV show that aired from 2011 to 2014, promises that you will consciously rise above your problems and your fears and live a better life.

When you make your opt-in page, I recommend using a product called AWeber. AWeber is an inexpensive way to collect people's names and emails from your registration page. Now you are done; you can start building your list.

Participants of our HeartCore Business programs, such as PACE, build a list consisting of 1,700–2,300 names on average.

OTHER WAYS OF BUILDING YOUR LIST

There are other ways to build your list in addition to the reporter model. One way is to pay $2–4 per lead on Facebook. That would cost you between $3,400 and $9,200 to build a list the size of the reporter model. However, that sum does not include the cost of having a Facebook team run your advertisements for you to target your ideal client. You also need to know how to market on Facebook to get a proper client.

When you pay $2–4 per lead on Facebook, you upload your existing list on Facebook and retarget those people and their friends. This is a warmer market. If you do it without using an existing list, your cost from Facebook marketing can be extraordinary high, and they could be untargeted. That is why you first want to build the list.

I do not recommend that you promote your reporter model series on Facebook. I have never been able to do it successfully without an excessive cost. The reporter model will cost between $1,200 and $1,400. That includes the technology, which is just AWeber, and the virtual assistant you can hire on HireMyMom.com.

I just saved you a ton of money by showing you how to build an audience the easy and most targeted way. It could be described as the virtual way of word-of-mouth, and word-of-mouth has repeatedly been proven to be the most successful conversion in sales.

There are still other ways to build your list. You can grow your audience by podcasts, Facebook advertisements, Twitter, Instagram (which I love), and other social media sites. All these are second-based strategies, meaning that I recommend all of them, but not when you first get started. Take the 90 days and buildout the list according to the reporter model.

Once you have a proper cash flow, you can hire specialists in the other social media platforms. They can teach you how to develop those areas, or you can let them do it for you. You do not need to become an expert on all the platforms. What you do need is to get cash in the door and free up your time.

◆◆◆

CHAPTER 6

GUARANTEED SALES SUCCESS

S top thinking that you already know what your audience or your list wants. It is an egocentric way of running a business, and it will cost you a lot of money and time. I want you to sell what your audience wants, not what you guess they want. If you have not surveyed your list, which we taught you how to build in the previous chapter, you will run into some challenges when it comes to conversion and putting real money in the bank.

A few years ago, I thought that my audience, the people on my list, wanted to learn about Internet marketing. It was based on what I heard from my existing clients. However, when I surveyed my list, I found that my audience wanted to learn about blogging.

I do not know what was influencing the marketplace at that time. But we are connected globally, and the media influences the minds of our ideal clients. We tend to think that we are individual thinkers. The truth is that we are influenced by the masses on a daily basis.

Without my survey, I would never have known that my audience wanted information about blogging. I turned around and put a strong emphasis on that, and we sold out.

When I did a survey the next year, the audience for blogging was small. Now they were interested in finding more clients.

I think that had a lot to do with the fact that many were running small and medium businesses and were operating mainly on a word-of-mouth marketing approach. Then the economy dropped, and they began to suffer. They did not have their customers in their databases, so they were not able to email them, build a relationship with them, and influence them on a regular basis. As people's bank accounts started drying up, the referral source also began drying up.

You want to survey your list every year, and you want to build your list once or twice a year. If you want to be successful, these need to be ongoing activities in your company.

Before you create the survey, I want you to think about what solution-driven product or service you want to sell. For instance, say you do real estate investments. Then you might build your list on the topic of investing on a budget.

After you have decided which solution-driven product or service you want to sell, you consider what you want from it. Here is where you get to dream a little. Maybe you have always wanted an investment group, and maybe your "why" is you want to network with investors around the world. Or maybe you want to learn from other people, or you want to make real estate investing a lifelong strategy for you to become financially free. Maybe you have a love and passion for it. Or maybe you just want to get into the market for the first time, and you want to have a network support group around you. It does not matter what it is; what matters is that you are clear about your why, because that is what will keep you in the game when things get hard.

If you follow the reporter model, you should go to Amazon and find people who have written books on the subject. If the topic is real estate investing, it could be authors, such as Robert Kiyosaki, Robert Allen, Russ Whitney, and "no names"—people who are popular but are not mass-market names. Believe it or not, it is many of the "no names" who can pull the greatest amount of people to your list.

Once you have found your 21 experts, you do the interview series about real estate investing on a budget. After you have built your list, you create your survey based on the product that you want to sell. Then you send out the survey to find out what your audience wants.

HOW TO CREATE A SURVEY

We use an inexpensive and wonderful online product called SurveyMonkey for our surveys. You need to create eight questions. The first seven questions are multiple choice with no comment box. It is a big mistake to put a feedback or comment box on your first seven questions. You want to force the subscribers to make a choice and tell you what they prefer. Based on the answers you receive to your multiple-choice questions, you create a product.

The eighth question is where you can ask them if there is anything more that they want you to know about them, if there is anything that you have missed, or if they would like to comment. There you create a comment box.

The notes left in the comment box are a great resource for ideas for newsletters, blogs, video content, and so on. You can also use the comments for online marketing. Then you do not have to worry about creating content; you can use the content that the subscribers gave you in the comment boxes.

If we continue with our example of an investment group, here are some examples of survey questions.

1. What makes you nervous about real estate investing?

    a) You have never done it before.

    b) Finding the money to invest.

    c) Losing your savings account.

    d) Not knowing how to find the right product to buy.

2. Why do you want more information about real estate investing?

    a) You want to quit your job and become a full-time real estate investor.

    b) It is your idea of creating a retirement fund.

    c) You have a passion for investing real estate.

    d) You want to create a network of more real estate-minded people around you.

You will see an overwhelming response to one answer to each question. That will tell you how you position your marketing and your language, and what points to address when selling your product.

Here is a sample of a real survey that I have done. **http://www.heartcorebusiness.com/survey**

When you create a survey, think of the things that you have to know. You want to create a product that you want to sell. What are the things that you would have to know about someone to be able to create the perfect product or the perfect plan for your new audience?

Brainstorm some of the problems that people can have that would make them unsuccessful. What are the problems that most people run into?

Here is another example: If you were going to create a Facebook marketing product, what would make a Facebook marketing campaign unsuccessful? It would be unsuccessful if it had no followers or a proper list. It would be unsuccessful if people did not understand your point of view or if you were afraid of or bad at selling.

After you have brainstormed, you can create your multiple-choice questions on those thoughts. Here is an example question.

1. What is your biggest challenge with marketing on Facebook?
   a) You have no friends or followers on Facebook.
   b) You do not know what to sell on Facebook.
   c) You do not know how to place a marketing ad on Facebook.

We try to find what the audience wants and identify what challenges they have. Perhaps they said that they have no friends on Facebook. Then, if you missed the part about showing them how to make friends in your product, you would have a product that would not work because you assumed they all had friends. Therefore, your buyer would have too many objections and would not buy.

Do not guess what people want, and do not start with creating a product. Start with building an audience list, and then survey that audience. Create a solution-based product or service that brings you millions of dollars in income and more free time.

CHAPTER 7

IT IS TIME TO CREATE BUZZ

Now it is time to create buzz about your product or service.

CHOOSE A BUSINESS MODEL

You can choose between two business models. If you like to control your product and service, and you want to own your company, you can sell your own product or service. This is a company model. If you have no desire to build an infrastructure of a business, you can sell somebody else's product or sell a multilevel marketing (MLM) product. This is an affiliate model. Both the company model and the affiliate model are great.

My family has a strong background in multilevel marketing. It is an excellent model for learning how to sell, and it allows you to get in with a low investment. However, you do not own that business.

Selling somebody else's product is great if you find it difficult to make decisions, or you think that you do not have enough credit or education to create your own business.

If perfectionism prevents you from getting started, or if you do not have a qualified product or service to sell, then go ahead and join a multilevel marketing company or sell somebody else's product from ClickBank.com.

Think of this whole process like going to the university. Only this time, you will get a return on your investment quickly. You should earn significantly more money than you invest in building your company in the first year in business.

It does not matter whether you sell your product or somebody else's product at this stage. What matters is that you learn the process, because once you learn it, you are golden. You can rinse and repeat the process and live out all your wildest dreams. Then, you can create the company that you want, and you will not be afraid or hesitant about it. You will just do it, which is the key to success.

THE LONG-TERM STRATEGY: KEEP THE CONNECTION

Once you have decided on a business model, you need to warm up your connection to your audience list. "Connection is currency." The owner of Zappos online shoe source said that many years ago, and I have never forgotten it.

- Connection is love.
- Connection is friendship.
- Connection with your body is fitness and health.
- You need a connection to make money.

You need to build that connection with your audience list. To do that, I recommend creating what is called an influencer campaign.

There are two things you need to think about in an influencer campaign: the long-term strategy and the short-term sales strategy. You start with the long-term strategy. The long-term vision is missed all the time, and entrepreneurs become lazy in this regard because they are chasing making money. The long-term strategy is to keep your connection to your list warm. That is why, once you build your list, you need to influence that list on an *ongoing weekly basis*. On the same day every single week, you need to send out a newsletter. You can send out more than one, but you need to be consistent with one.

The reason many people love Starbucks is because it is consistent; you know what you are going to get when you go to Starbucks, whether you go in Bali, Indonesia, or Del Mar, California. It always has the same feel, energy, and customer service.

When you run a virtual business, a huge part of what you need to do is create a similar trust, like, and love. You do that by being consistent with a weekly newsletter.

To put together good information for your weekly newsletter, go back to your SurveyMonkey, and use topics that came up in the survey's comment section. In addition, search the Internet for statistics and articles, and mix them in with your opinion. For instance, I love *Inc.* magazine and *Fast Company*, and I read them on a regular basis. I will read an article there, and then I write a review of it in my newsletter. Or an article might stimulate an opinion from me that I can write about. It will influence my list of people and make them think, and that brings us into a virtual dialogue.

If you send out a newsletter where the readers have to click to get the steps or more information, or the bulk of the article is on your blog, this teaches your audience to click to buy. And this is also how you have ongoing virtual communication with them, which creates a connection.

On your blog, ask your readers for comments and feedback. Ask them what they liked about it and what they did not like. By doing so, you create an ongoing conversation. Then make sure that you respond to those conversations so that you build a relationship with them.

THE SHORT-TERM STRATEGY: A THREE-VIDEO SERIES

The second strategy is your influencer selling campaign. Before you sell your product, you need to influence your audience and build a deeper relationship with them. This is where you create the buzz about your product or service.

I recommend that you make a three-video series. Once you have collected information from the survey that you sent out, create three, 15 to 30-minute long videos on your theme. Many people think that their websites are about education. However, they are not. Your blogs, emails, and videos are where you educate and influence. The primary purpose of your website is not to have people look through all your products and services but to collect their data. You want to collect their data so you can send them your offers and education via email.

I recommend everybody to make videos. In the first video, you want to set the context or the vision or open possibilities. You want to inspire and excite your viewers about what you will teach them in the videos.

For instance, say I am a business coach, and I discover from my survey that many people are interested in learning how to build a business that within two years allows them to quit their jobs and make $30,000 to $50,000 a month. The problem for people in my audience is that they do not have much time, because they have another job, and they do not know the step-by-step plan to get to their goals.

Then the name of my three-video series might be, "Step-by-Step Plan to Make $30,000 to $50,000 a Month Working from Home, Even If You Have a Job or Kids."

- **Video 1.** In the first video, you need to show them how this is possible. This is a great place to share a story that proves your point. The story could be your own or somebody else's. You need to help them see that their dream is possible. Then you need to hook them to make sure that they will keep a lookout for the second video, which will come the following day.

- **Video 2.** The second video needs to be full of information about how to do it. In my case example, I might give five to seven steps about how to build the list, survey it, and convert it, so they can make the $30,000 to $50,000 a month within two years, even if they have a job or kids at home. The second video builds trust, like, and love. You can also add a worksheet that you ask them to fill out. It will make them more engaged, and engagement is good. That means they are not tuning out. They are tuning in. Then you hook them for the third video. It is easy. Trust yourself. The more certain you are and the stronger your leadership skills are, the more you will be able to persuade your viewers to pursue your offer.

- **Video 3.** The third video is where you handle all their objections. I might say something like, "In the first video, I showed you how it's possible. In the second video, I showed you how to do it. In the third video, I want to talk about the three things that can prevent you from doing it. I will also point out the areas where I see entrepreneurs face challenges and end up not applying the coaching and training that I gave you in the second video. Let's talk about that now. The first thing that prevents entrepreneurs from being successful is they try to do it all on their own. They do not seek the support of a coach or mentor or hire a virtual assistant to help them."

Then I would discuss how to find a good coach. It is not necessarily a sales pitch, because you are not trying to sell to them here. Your focus is to help them.

If you put your clients or your potential clients in the forefront to win, most of them will make the choice to work with you. If you make the mistake of pushing your services and your products on them in this video, and you try to sell too quickly, you become a sleazy salesperson.

There needs to be a balance; you do not want your viewers to be indecisive, and you do not want them to want you to leave them alone. You want them to feel attracted to you and trust you. We trust people who help us. We do not trust people who are out to fend for themselves. Do not be that person.

Then I would go on in the video to share the second and third most common objections or problems. At the end of the third video, you could do one of two things. First, if you think you need more time with your audience, you could lead them to a 90-minute educational conference call. You want the topic of the conference call to be different from your three-video series. I would not discuss the topic of making $30,000 to $50,000 a month during the 90-minute conference call. I would pick an entirely different theme.

Go back to the information from the survey and pick another topic based on that. It could be something that they are interested in, or it could be a solution to a particular problem. Then teach, train, or talk about that on the call.

We recommend that all our clients take that extra step and do the 90-minute conference call, but you do not have to.

Second, you could give your audience an opportunity to speak with you. Insert a URL or a button on the page where they watch the video that gives them an opportunity to receive advice from you.

I would advise you to offer coaching or consultation at a fee between $27 and $67 to speak with you or someone on your team. This is what is called a sales lead offer. Anybody who takes money out of their pocket is a more qualified buyer, and they are more committed to your topic.

You need to tell your audience the value of that call. For instance, I might say, "I do not offer the public an opportunity to receive coaching from me for one hour only. You can work with me for five hours on a VIP day, on a one-year mentorship program, or in different communities or groups that we run with other master trainers, depending on what your needs are."

If I were to offer a strategy session where someone could speak with me or one of my business coaches for $67, I would let my audience know that this is an offer they cannot miss. I would let them know that if they want coaching from me or my team, it typically costs from $7,000 to $40,000, depending on the access level, and they would have to commit for a year. That makes the $67 offer extremely valuable, and people understand that value.

Whenever somebody has a monetary objection, it is not because they do not have the money. They will spend it somewhere else, if not with you. If they have a monetary issue, it is because they do not see the value. You have to excel at articulating the value of something in a language that your audience can understand.

From the third video, you can lead your viewers right to a paid strategy session with you or somebody on your staff. Or you can let them know to keep their eyes open because you will have a 90-minute conference call, training call, webinar, or something similar, about a topic that you have pulled from the survey. This will create the connection and the buyers you are looking for, and you will start making a significant amount of money from your list without waiting for long.

IN SUMMARY

It takes 90 days to build an audience list. Once you have built your list, you must survey it. After you survey that list, you move to the step we just discussed, which is creating the buzz about your product or service.

It is important that you do it without getting caught up in the thinking stage of the process. Do not procrastinate trying to make it perfect. Just do it. And remember to think of this process like you are going to a university, but being paid to become educated.

If you are the type of person who needs more details, you are welcome to reach out to us at HeartCoreBusiness.com. We are here to serve. We have many qualified business coaches, and I take many of the calls myself. We are happy to help support you on your journey to success.

◆

CHAPTER 8

CREATING YOUR OWN ECONOMY

In this chapter, I will show you some numbers that will illustrate where you convert sales and make money so that you create the freedom that you want.

As you read this book and build your business, it is critical that you tap into the fact that every single one of us has a core calling. There is a drastic difference between building a business to make money and developing a core calling.

I have worked with thousands of entrepreneurs and corporate executives. The one thing that remains true is that if you do not want to burn out, you need to do something that is a core calling of yours. It needs to be something that keeps pulling you forward, like a voice inside you, nagging you to pay attention.

When I was a young girl, I had a desire to be like life and business strategist Tony Robbins. And today, the one thing I love to do is to coach. One of my girlfriends is a singer. She has opened for singer/songwriter Shania Twain, and she has emceed for some of the best authors in the world. It always comes back to the one thing she loves to do, which is to sing.

You also have a core calling. But it is likely that you have ignored it for a long time or perhaps taken a couple of steps toward it but shelved it to focus on doing something that will take care of the bills, make money, and provide you with financial security.

The challenge is that when you work without following your core calling, you always hit a wall. It could be that you lose your health or your job, or it could be that you have no passion for what you are doing, which ripples into unhappiness.

As you read this book, I want you to be cautious that you do not follow these steps solely to make money, which they will do for you! What I will show you about creating your own economy is a process that you can rinse and repeat once you have built your list and studied everything that I am teaching you.

This book is not just a theory book. It tells you how to do it. You might need extra coaching or mentoring for some of the details or for holding yourself accountable. But the truth is that everything you read here will make you money. No steps are left out. However, if you do not follow these steps toward your core calling, you will hit a wall.

It is time to stop muting the nagging voice inside you—the calling that you have wanted to respond to for a long time. Do not give up because you do not know how to make money with it, how to package it, or how to (fill in the blank). Instead, you must have the grit to pass that stopping point and seek the help you need to identify your core calling, develop it, and make the money that you want.

At this point, you have built your list and done your survey, and you now have the data from that survey. In the last chapter, I taught you how to create buzz about your products and service based on the information you collected.

Now, let's discuss what you offer. How do you package your product or service so that it shows you the money?

BEGIN AT THE RIGHT END

Most online marketers and advertising specialists will want to sell something that is at a low price point. There is a strategy to that, and it works. When you first offer your audience a product or service at a low price point, you find a more qualified buyer. Anybody who will take $2, $5, or $27 out of their pocket to buy a report, a book, etcetera, is a more committed buyer than somebody who only takes something from you for free. So, there is a strategy to first selling the low-price product, but that it not what we do when we follow my Freedom Model.

If you are like the average entrepreneur who I see on a daily basis, you will build a list consisting of 1,700–2,300 people. To become wealthy and financially free with a low price point offer, it will take you a significantly bigger list than that. That means it will take more time on your part to get off the ground and get a proper income.

I want you to make six figures in your first year in business. In your second year, I want to see you move to the $200,000 and $300,000 mark. After that, I want you to start hitting the half-million-dollar mark and the one-million-dollar mark. For you to do that, you need to follow my Freedom Model, which means that the first thing you sell is a high-end product.

The high-end product is what will make you financially stable. It is what will make it possible for you to quit your other job if you want to. It will enable you to pay your bills and be financially secure.

I have not found any other model in any industry that will make you financially free this quickly. People who follow other models constantly tell you that you will be out of pocket in your first year in business, but that is not true. You will not be out of pocket if you follow this model.

You can turn almost any business into a coaching or consulting business because, in every field, there are people who want advice. I am going to use the coaching model or the consulting model as an example so that you can see how the numbers add up.

Let's say you start your coaching business, and you sell the high-end product first. You begin by charging each client $800 per month, which is not even a high price point. Most skilled coaches charge between $3,000 and $5,000 per month by years two to three of their careers. But let's start there, because I do not know what your sales skills are yet.

If you need to improve your sales skills, take two seconds now and go to HeartCoreBusiness.com. We have a Cash Flow program that will teach you how to close $10,000 or $20,000 deals in 15-minute conversations over the phone. Do not struggle through and try to guess how to do it, because it is your path to financial freedom.

Now, let's say the result of your list building was 1,500 new people on your list. If you provide two hours of coaching and consulting time to ten people and charge each $800 per month, you will make $8,000 per month. While you continue in your corporate job, you can sell that on the side for a couple of months without wearing out yourself. And now you have $96,000 for your annual income.

The great thing is that you do not have a lot of marketing costs in the beginning, because there are no large costs attached to building and surveying your list. All you need is a computer, an Internet connection, and a phone. You can work on the beaches of Greece if you want.

You now work 20 hours each month with 10 clients, and you make $96,000 a year. Does that sound like a picture to freedom? It does to me. Maybe it's not yet as much money as you want to earn, but you can see how quickly that turnaround is from your list build to two months of selling to $96,000. There is no stock or real estate investment that will ever give you a higher return than what you can do with your own money and time.

THE PRODUCT THAT WILL MAKE YOU WEALTHY

After you have sold and mastered selling your high-end product or service to 10 private clients, I want you to move to selling a product or service at a medium price point.

The midrange product is what will give you leverage and make you wealthy. It is what the majority of your clients will want to buy, because this is the commitment level where most people are. It is the easiest program or product to sell, and it often makes the biggest difference.

Let's continue the idea of the coaching or consulting model. Say it took you two months to sell your high-end service while you worked at your other job, and you now make $96,000 each year. At this point, take three months off selling. Get used to having these 10 new clients. This is how you create peace and balance so that you can enjoy your life and family. Celebrate your victories. There is no rush to become financially free because with this plan, you can do it within two years or so.

After three months, you begin selling the midrange service. This time, allow yourself three months to sell to 30 people (sell 10 people per month). For the medium price point, you charge each client $400 per month. You now make an additional $12,000 per month and $144,000 per year. Between both products, you will earn a total of $240,000 during your first two years in business, and your overhead is almost nothing. Think about what is possible if you listen to your core calling and put it into a model like this.

If you do not know how to go about this, I encourage you to reach out to me or another coach or businessperson you trust who can help you because these numbers are extremely doable.

Here is a text message that I got from a woman who has been in business for two-and-a half years.

"This is my first 100K sales month. Feels SO good!!!! I added 8 clients into my group, which totals $53,792 in sales. And I added 4 new private clients. 2 pay in full and 2 installments for a total of $51,200 in sales."

THE SECRET OF THE LOW-END PRODUCT

Last comes the lower price point. We use a low price point strategy to qualify more leads. You spent some dollars to purchase this book, meaning you are more committed than the average person to develop your dream and achieve financial freedom. But if you follow the Freedom Model, you will not sell the low-end product first. You will sell it last. You can use Facebook strategies or your list to sell a fantastic product at a low price point.

You will probably not do this in your first year in business, as there is no need. I have shown you how to sell $240,000 in your first year if you hustle, so you should be happy. That can easily multiply to millions if you just choose to follow that strategy.

The secret to selling a great product at a low price point is to have a thorough knowledge of your audience. The best way for you to know your audience properly is if you have worked closely with 20 people.

As you buildout your business this year, continue allowing yourself the space and time to enjoy your life. Maintain balance. Enjoy the beaches, go on a vacation, love up your lover, and create a quality life while you get to know your clients properly. As you get to know them, take the one thing that is imperative to them and sell it at a low price point. It allows you to identify the people who are genuinely committed. You can upsell them into a higher program, product, or service.

As I am writing this book, we are selling "How to Close a Sales Conversation in 15 Minutes." It is not my Cash Flow program, which is six hours of some of the best sales training you will ever come across. But online, we sell the sales conversation as a 15–20 minute video at a low price point.

We also offer a PDF called "Risk Management Follow Up Series." This plan gives a step-by-step formula for what to do if somebody does not say yes or if somebody says no. It shows you how to follow up, which is important, considering the fact that 60 percent of your money will come from follow-up conversations.

In addition, you receive a 30-minute coaching session with one of the HeartCore Business coaches. We do not sell individual coaching sessions, so you cannot buy this service on our website.

The only other way you can work with me or any of my coaches is through a one-year program. That is our business model, because you need to know where your cash flow is coming from. But most important, it is because I know that I cannot make a big difference in your life with one call. I need to work with you between one and three years to get you to where you want to be. If I let you go as a client before you see results, what do you think happens? You will not refer other clients to me.

Make sure that you think about your company's long-term plan, not just a short-term plan. It is critical that we help you get the results you want because if we do not, our company implodes. I want you to think about your company the same way.

We know what our clients at HeartCore Business struggle with the most, so we offer the snippet of my sales conversation, the follow-up risk management plan, and the 30-minute coaching session with one of the HeartCore Business coaches, all for $7. The value of that package is probably about $1,000. People all over the world have used my 15-minute sales conversation strategy to close $7,000, $10,000, and more deals on the phone with their audience and cold leads from Facebook. That is why my sales conversation easily is worth $1,000. It can even be worth $20,000 once you have closed that amount in your business.

Our low-end product funnels people into our midrange product, which is the equivalent of the program at $400 per month that I discussed earlier.

Quickly accessing freedom does not take great talent or many skills. There is light at the end of the tunnel, even if you do not possess great business skills. If you do possess great business skills, the Freedom Model will allow you to earn money relatively quickly.

If you have the courage to follow your core calling, there is freedom at the end of this road. You do not have to struggle. You do not have to work where you do not want to. And you do not have to chase the mighty dollar to survive. The secret is having enough courage to read a book like this, put what you read into action, have enough grit to see it all the way through, and not stop until you get there.

The numbers that I have described to you should be motivation enough. The short time it takes to do it should open your eyes to the possibility that you might be working too hard. All you need to do is build the list, survey that list, and use the sales model that I just laid out for you to move your life toward financial freedom.

◆◆◆

CHAPTER 9

TEAM SUPPORT

B efore we talk about building out the team, I want to remind you about the goal of the Freedom Model. The Freedom Model is a plan where the goal is to replace yourself in your business and make the income that you want so that you can enjoy the life that you desire.

FREEDOM MODEL

LIST BUILD

HIGH END → MID → LOW END

SKILL: MASTER SALES

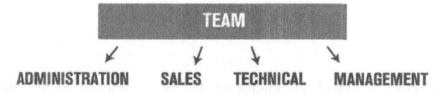

TEAM

ADMINISTRATION → SALES → TECHNICAL → MANAGEMENT

SKILL: LEADERSHIP - WHO ARE YOUR "LIFER" EMPLOYEES?

GET KNOWN

YOU CEO

REPLACE YOURSELF → OPERATIONS → HUMAN RESOURCES

SKILL: SELLING WITHOUT YOU; DOING FULFILLMENT 401K, HEALTH INSURANCE, LIFELONG

BIGGER VISION
The reason you Became an Entrepreneur in the First Place
TIME TO BECOME THE FACE PERSON OF YOUR COMPANY

It takes about two years for you to become comfortable with your business and for your business to make good money. Replacing yourself, however, takes five years.

I believe people become entrepreneurs because they want the freedom lifestyle. But most never make it because they do not understand the entire Freedom Model. Depending on your goals and dreams, keep that in mind as you read and implement the ideas in this book about how to make it happen.

Let's now discuss how to build a team—staff or group of contractors—in such a way that they stay with you forever. "Forever" is a term that I use loosely. If someone stays with you for three to five years and then leaves your company, that should be a big quantum leap that takes your company to the next level. You are only going to improve hiring and spotting great talent, and you are only going to become less tolerant of bad labor.

Finding good help is probably one of the biggest challenges that entrepreneurs face. Unfortunately, corporate America does not breed strong teams to work for small-sized or medium-sized businesses. Many people in corporate America just collect paychecks, and if you were to follow them around, you would see that they are not productive.

I say that because I was in corporate America for many years. I know how hard I worked, and I also know how many times I slacked off, how many times I took longer lunches, and how many times I was unengaged in what I was doing. I was surfing the Internet or looking at Facebook. I say that from a humble and transparent place. When somebody pays your bills, it is a lot easier to be unproductive because your ass is not on the line.

How do you find the small percentage of people who take great pride in what they do and strive to be successful?

First, you need to understand your value system and what is important to you. If you hire somebody who does not have the same value system as you, you are in trouble.

My two highest values are economics and community. I am generous to a fault. Because I love to create a family, community, and team, I have had to train myself to not overpay people and to make them work for what they earn in my company. That is part of the Freedom Model and part of what is going to help you be wildly successful and not break the bank along the way.

If you are an entrepreneur, there is a good chance that you also highly value economics—you long to become financially free. As you are reading this book, you want a freedom lifestyle. A huge part of a freedom lifestyle is having the income to do what you want when you want to do it.

If you hire people who do not highly value economics or do not have a high work ethic, then you will become frustrated. You will end up pulling them across the finish line and managing them in a way that will cause you more harm than good. You will take care of the business instead of allowing other people to do their jobs for you, which is a big mistake that entrepreneurs make.

Starting entrepreneurs try to do all the tech work, sales, and graphics themselves. Some of them like it. They like to geek out with graphics and create banners and little tasks like that. However, it makes more financial sense to go to online sites and pay a freelance graphic designer to design your banner. You have to learn how to allow a team to support you so that you have more open time in the day.

The same applies to your personal life. I love cleaning my house and detailing my car, but I had to let go of those activities to build my company. There was not enough time. If it is my day off, and if I am cleaning the house, what am I not doing? I am not exercising. I am not making love to my man. I am not spending time with my son and my girlfriends. Let go of the things that nobody cares about. People don't care about who washes the floor. They care about quality time. They care about you being present.

You need to apply this logic and be conscious as you develop your business. When you let go of control, you will be supported to grow.

WHOM TO HIRE AND WHEN

The first year in your business, you only need an admin or a virtual assistant. You should focus on expanding your team in the second year. That year, you need to make team building the theme.

As we discussed previously, the admin team is the first team you need to have in place. Second is your sales team. Third is your tech team. Fourth is your operations manager or HR, depending on what you need most in your business.

Let's begin by discussing how to hire a good admin who can help you build your business. Usually when you start a business, you need an admin who understands how to put up a registration page online, maybe upload a blog online, and send out emails.

Interviewing people takes a lot of time, which is what we try to avoid in the Freedom Model. So, before you interview people, you create a test for them. A test could be setting up a registration page. You want to send the test to them on a Friday afternoon and see how long it takes them to get it back to you. If they get it back to you within one or two hours, you have found somebody who is ambitious and cares about getting the job.

Somebody who responds to you three or four days later, after the weekend, is typically someone who is not urgent about getting that job. The way somebody does one thing is the way they do everything. If you hire the person who is not urgent, he or she will let you down. It will be difficult to get that person to help you drive your company to where you need it to be during the next two to five years. You need somebody who is driven, somebody who is a bit of a workaholic. Then you can pull that person back instead of trying to push that person forward.

The second thing you want to do when you interview people is talk to them about being with your company for the next three to five years. Then you set a long-term goal with them, and you can find out if that is even interesting to them. Far too many entrepreneurs hire assistants, or virtual assistants, just to get themselves off the ground, and they treat their employees almost like they were numbers rather than real people.

Instead of treating new employees like servants, you want them to feel like they are a piece of the company so that they feel like they have ownership. They need to know that they are a big part of bringing your company to where it needs to be, because they are. You cannot do it alone.

The admin you hire needs to be organized. He or she should have urgency and attention to detail. Ask a question, such as, "If I looked in your bedroom right now, what would I see?" Perhaps they tell you that they have clothes all over the floor and two-day-old tomato soup on their nightstand. Maybe they giggle and say, "I would be a little embarrassed if you walked into my room." Even if you are a messy person, that is not somebody you want to hire, because your admin has to organize your business and get things done in a timely manner.

Create another couple of personal questions that you might want to ask in the interview. Those questions will allow you to determine the attitude of the person, which is more important than the talents of the person, because talents can be taught.

You also might want to ask what their last goal was and if they hit it. Look for answers like, "Yes, I hit it." Then you ask them, "What's a goal you haven't hit, and how did you deal with that?" If their answer is "Well, life just happens and you don't hit all your goals," you do not want that person. They do not possess enough economic drive to be a support team for an entrepreneur. You want them to say something like, "I just recommit and go after it again." You need somebody who already has drive, if you want them to help you be successful and build your company so that you achieve your freedom lifestyle.

The second team you add is your sales team. Ideally, your sales team is current customers or clients who you hire. Hiring customers or clients from within is the fastest way to double sales in your company, because they are already sold on your product. We have always hired clients to sell for us, and we have taught them how to sell. We have taught the Cash Flow program, which teaches people how to sell in 15-minute conversations, to our entire client base. Then I, as a CEO, become the coach and the cheerleader, helping the sales team earn money and make a difference.

We incentivize our sales team by giving them a percentage of their closes. We also give them a disclosure, because we have such a high success rate in our business-coaching program that our ideal client matches a certain criterion. If they speak to somebody who we cannot help, they do not make them an offer. However, in PACE or our Marketing Mastery program, we can help most people that our sales team speaks to. They will always begin by helping you, and if you are a good fit, they will make you an offer. If you are not, they refer you to someone who is a better fit.

The entire sales team has participated in my Cash Flow program. If you need to enhance your skills in sales or train a team, the Cash Flow program is an excellent product for you.

If you cannot hire people for your sales team from within, there are other ways that also work. You can, for example, find a sales team via online searches. However, it is not my favorite way. I would rather use the experiences and wins of our clients to sell our products. They transfer energy when they talk to people because they firmly believe in what we do, and that certainty comes across when they speak to a potential client. In turn, they close more sales for our company. But, of course, it is your choice.

Third, comes your tech team. Remember, we are in year two when we establish this team. The priority of your tech team is to take some pressure off your admin and start doing some of your online marketing. At this point, the primary focus of the tech and marketing team will be to automate lead generation. Then you bring in new potential clients every day without doing the reporter model, the interview series. You should still do the reporter model twice a year. In between, a new business should be growing its list from 500 to 2,000 people each month with an automated system.

Your tech team is responsible for growing the automated lead generation system. We use Facebook. It is our strongest lead generation, because we can target different cities, and we can target specific demographics, likes, and dislikes.

The fourth and final addition to your team is an operations manager or HR department. It will probably not be added in your second year but maybe closer to your fourth year. It sets you up to remove yourself from project management of your company, and it gives you enough knowledge about how to run your company. Make sure you have one clear objective for the management position. Hire for the specific job to get a particular job done and relieve you of pressure.

HELP YOUR TEAM TO GROW

To develop your team the best way, *the first step* is to read *The One Minute Manager*, as referenced in Chapter 3. This book will teach you how to stop being a controller and stop picking up all the tasks of the people who work for you. It will also teach you how to empower your employees to do their jobs and not need you for every single answer. Then your inbox will start to clear up, and people will become self-empowered.

I recommend also reading the book with your staff. Once a week, discuss the chapters that people are reading and how you can implement or do better as a company to be more self-empowered as department heads, including your assistant.

The second step is to hire every person on your team with a three-year to five-year vision. Nobody is a temporary employee. Everybody is a part of a vision of growing bigger. You need to know what each person on your team would love to do in your company. Your job is continually to put that reward in front of them so that they can keep progressing and growing. Money is not the best motivation, but progress is. If your team members' visions are bigger or entail more responsibility than the position they are in now, they will move forward. Then they will be in their most motivated state, which is being valuable.

The third step is to know your two top values. Mine are economics and team, meaning money and community/family. What do you value most in life? If you are unsure, look at your bank statements for the last three months, and you will see what you are most committed to.

The fourth step is to pay low and grow high. As I said, I am generous to a fault. I have ruined many great employees by paying them too much in the beginning. Consider having a 90-day trial and let people grow into the incomes that they want to make based on them increasing the sales volume in your company. As you grow and win, reward them along the way. We have some of the highest paid sales people, admin support, and employees. They have worked with me for two or three years, plus they deserve every dollar they receive. They also receive substantial bonuses.

I recently met somebody in the tech field in San Diego, who received a $900 bonus from her company after having worked for them for six years. I understand that there are many employees and that bonuses are expensive for the company. But I also know that your company would never look the way it looks, make the amount of money it makes, and run as well as it runs without the team.

Give your team generous bonuses and take care of them. We give many of our team members bonuses of $3,000 to $5,000. At Christmas time, we send their families unique gifts that make them feel special and loved. We make sure that we know the love language of everybody on our team, and we give them what we know is important to them and what motivates them.

All our team members are motivated differently. For instance, one of my trainers is highly motivated by wine and food. If I send her a $200 bottle of wine or make a reservation and pay for her dinner at a restaurant that might have a six-month waiting list, that is over the top for her. She loves it. I have another person on my team who is more motivated by recognition than money. What make her feel important are awards, being highlighted in front of the company, and more authoritative decision making. To keep your team members motivated and have them be productive, you must find out what is important to each of them.

Look for creative ways to pay lower bases and higher commissions to your team. Obviously, it does not work for every position. It does not work for your admin, but it does work for your sales team, coaches, and consultants.

People who work in the real estate industry, brokers, salespeople, or even financial advisors are, for the most part, responsible for finding their own leads to being in the top percentage of their industry.

If you follow the Freedom Model when you build your business, and you provide leads to your team, then you can pay them anywhere from 10 to 20 percent commissions. As a result, they can earn insane amounts of money. We have people who earn $100,000 annually in their second year of working with us. They do not have to spend any money on marketing; they have no risk on the table, and they work part-time. That is because they receive a good commission structure as far as helping us when we have events, sales campaigns, launches, or programs.

Look for ways to replicate that. This is yet another way to make sure that the people in your organization are driven. People in your organization are now making a recurring income based on sales volume. It makes the team work together, and the team that works together jells together.

As entrepreneurs, especially owners of small or medium businesses, we are often afraid to let go of some of our not-so-good staff or contractors because we think we need them.

I will never forget meeting Bert Jacobs, one of the brothers who owns the Life Is Good clothing company. When I talked to Bert, his company was at about the $100 million mark and growing. I will always remember what he said to me. He said, "Shanda, I have never regretted firing or letting go somebody in my organization. Whenever you feel that somebody is not a good fit, you need to trust your instincts and let them go quickly. Hire slow. Fire fast."

Never allow yourself to be hostage to somebody who works for your company. Always find a way that you can use contractors or virtual people to plug the holes as you find the next ideal person to fill that position.

Far too many company owners experience slow growth because they tolerate people who have entitlement issues, or lack work ethic, or want more money than what the job description calls for. You need team members who will grow along with your company. They should believe in your vision and be rewarded and taken care of by you as the company grows.

Every time Bert let somebody go, he always found a better person for that job. Trust the flow. Trust the fact that everything happens for a reason. When you have an inclination that somebody is not cutting it, then cut them.

◆◆◆

CHAPTER 10

BECOME AN INFLUENCER

You are now in the third year of your business. You are set to grow massively this year, so you should be excited. By now, your admin team and sales team are set. There are probably areas that you still want to improve, and that is fine. Make sure that you train your sales team properly or use our Cash Flow program to help them develop their sales skills.[1]

REPLACE YOURSELF

Moving forward in your third year, you need to focus on the person who is going to replace you. You want to train one main person for this task. During the next two years, you will let go of control and teach, coach, and mentor this person so that she or he can start replacing you. Eventually, she or he will breathe like you, answer the same way you do, and embody the culture like you do. Then, in the next phase, you can step into the position of driving the vision of your company and become

---

1   Cash Flow program can be ordered at http://www.heartcorebusiness.com.

its face. You have now created ultimate freedom. And this is the year that your company doubles in size.

Even though you pinpoint one person to succeed you, you also want to have a backup person. Something could easily happen to the person whom you intend to replace yourself with. They could get sick or hit by a car, or they could, for some odd reason, have a change of heart and decide that it is not going to work. Or you might realize halfway through the next year that this person is not able to replace you. You want to have a backup person so that your plan for the company always moves forward and never interferes with the life that you intend to create.

The skill that you need to develop now is letting go of control. Know that you are not the only person who can do your job and do it well. Talents can always be taught, and the people on the top are not the most talented ones. On top are the people who put in the most effort. You need to look for the person who has the right nonstop attitude to replace you. For instance, I invest anywhere from $5,000 to $20,000 in additional skill training for the person who will replace me, so that she or he becomes a better presenter, coach, and leader. That person is leading a huge training program for my company.

I invest in that person and a backup person in case something happens to my first choice. That way, I never have to step back into that role. Then I can keep taking on things without fearing that I might have to return and take over that division again. It is this mindset that you should adopt. Focus on moving toward your vision; do not focus on the fear of something going wrong.

BRAND YOUR COMPANY

In the third year, you need to start marketing your company differently. Now you transition from being the company to becoming the face of the company. This is normally a good time to invest in branding. At year three, people usually know what they are doing. They are not living with uncertainty. And hopefully, if they received good coaching, they are not floundering.

If you have followed the steps in this book, you now know what you are doing and what your core calling is. Branding your company will help you put the final touches on it. Proper branders will make you consistent. They will help you reach more people than before, and they will more than double your income this year. Branding is not just about a pretty logo or a sophisticated website. It is about the architecture, the messaging, and the organization of the entire internal guts of your company. It is your reputation!

The visuals are just the packaging. They are like the blue box that you receive when you buy a piece of jewelry at Tiffany & Co. The blue box is recognizable and an excellent brand. However, Tiffany as a company stands for something entirely different—a certain quality or specialness that no other jeweler can give you. It is not just the logo, and it is not just the packaging. It is the identity, the architecture, the guts, and the consistency that makes that brand reach far.

Many people mess up branding by doing it far too early. If you follow my model, the time to brand is about year three, when your company is making about $200,000 to $300,000 per year. If it is not, it does not matter how much you brand. It will not grow your company the way it will if you follow my model. Get your cash flow going first!

It is difficult to find a good brander. My personal recommendation is Re Perez and his company, Branding for the People. After having worked for huge firms, Re branched off with what he had learned from helping those firms explode in the market. He priced his service at price points that small and medium business owners could afford. He helps businesses take quantum leaps to reach more people. He also helps you create a desired brand and organize your thoughts to take your company to the next level.

The reason you want to brand your company is because it is time for you to become known. You are as ready as ever with the structures that you now have in place, even if you do not feel like it. This year is the time to double your income. Remember to keep building your audience list twice a year, and use the tech and marketing team to implement your online, targeted, automated, list building on a regular basis. In other words, keep building your list and add the branding component.

BECOME KNOWN

How do you become known? You want to become the face of your company.

The first way to become known is by attending quality charity events and doing good work online and off. Some of the most influential people are a part of charities.

Find a charity that you care about. For instance, I go to Africa and help women build businesses there. I also care a lot about the victims of human trafficking. Something about that resonates with my heart, and I feel passionate about making a difference in that arena.

Look for charities that call on your heart. Do not pick a charity just to network. That is worthless. Connection is what converts to currency, which means that connection is what will bring about more opportunities, and your network will always be your net worth.

You are the sum of the five people you are closest to. Most people need to find better friends. Why not find better friends by working with charities you care about? Then you already have a common interest, a common connection, which will create an authentic relationship. That will, in turn, lead to fantastic opportunities.

The second way to become known is through sponsorship. I have not yet met an entrepreneur who cannot create a keynote speech to speak to their ideal audience, whether it is TED Talk or events held by other entrepreneurs.

Sponsorship costs money. You need proper coaching about your presentation and your keynote, which ideally comes from a strategy coach, like we have at HeartCore Business. Sponsoring a proper event could cost you between $1,400 and $50,000. Of course, you do not invest in the bigger price points until you have a presentation that works well and converts well.

If you receive proper training and the right business advice, you can almost always double your sponsorship investment. If I invest $15,000 to speak on a stage for an hour, I will make $30,000 for that hour. That is how sponsorship works. It is worth your time. If you use it correctly, it will get you known in your field and to your client base.

The third way to become known is by speaking in your local town or city on a volunteer basis. For example, you can offer to speak at women's networking groups. Search online for organizations where your topic is relevant and ask if they bring in outside speakers. If they do, you can easily give free talks. While you are there, have a raffle or give something valuable for the purpose of collecting the data of the people in the room. Remember: Always be building your list.

Another option is speaking at virtual events, telesummits, video summits, live streams, and webinars. I have seen many financial advisors, lawyers, and attorneys use excellent webinar formats to educate the marketplace on their topics and to generate leads. All the speaking formats are great ways for you to become more known in your industry.

What makes you stand out and become known is having a loud point of view. That means that it is time for you to piss some people off. When you piss some people off, you also create raving fans! And whenever you create raving fans, you create haters. This is an excellent thing for business and a sign that you are making a difference!

When we receive hate mail in our organization, we send the email around and celebrate because we know that our point of view ruffled some feathers. If your point of view does not ruffle any feathers, you are too quiet and too safe. Being safe equals being broke. Your mother and father probably told you to keep your opinion to yourself and tone down a characteristic of yours. Now is the time to bring it out and make some money. Your point of view is what pays.

You have a good point of view, if it hits four different points.

- First, it needs to be concrete.
- Second, you must be able to say it within a maximum of two sentences.
- Third, it needs to be clear, not esoteric.
- Fourth, everyone you say it to needs to understand what you are talking about.

For instance, my point of view in HeartCore Business is that business is hard unless you put your marketing in the right order. Any point of view you will ever hear from me will be the same thing, because I am concrete, consistent, and clear. Everybody understands the language that I am using, and I can say it in one or two sentences.

My second point of view supports and follows my first point of view, which is that making money, saving money, and building your business are not more important than living your life. That is what the freedom lifestyle is all about. I can also say that you can retire five years after startup if you put your marketing in the right order. All of these are clear points of view, and if you reread them, you will realize they say the same thing.

If you dig deep down, you will realize that you already have a strong belief system about what your topic, your theme, or your product is. Do not allow yourself to get confused here, because most people have a meltdown when I talk about point of view at our event. Trust yourself and do not try to fit in. Be okay with a bunch of people disagreeing with you. When many people disagree with you, there are even more people who completely agree with you. That is your key to success.

◆◆◆

CHAPTER 11

HABITS

C hange your habits; change your life. That is the theme of this chapter. It is probably the most important chapter in this entire book. If you understand everything that I have spoken about—the marketing, the business plans, and what to focus on—then you should be wildly successful. But why are some people unsuccessful? It is because of their habits.

I have been the employee, the executive, the girlfriend, and the friend who always had a great idea in the beginning but never had what it took to finish my goal. I am sure that you are painfully aware of the habits that you have that prevent you from being more successful and having more money and freedom.

COMMON HABITS

A common bad habit of entrepreneurs is that they think they are the only ones who can do the job well, so they take on more tasks that steal their freedom! Those who are the most successful have let go of control to grow! Many will say, "Oh, well, they can do that because they have the money." No, that is incorrect. They let go of control while building their company, and that is why they have the freedom, creativity, great ideas, and energy to execute their plans.

Another bad habit that is common among entrepreneurs is that they will not release a product or start a project until they have perfected it. Perfectionism is the sister of procrastination. You will always see those two sisters hanging out together. It is an extremely bad habit of entrepreneurs who stay in the rat race and burn out. Nothing you ever create will be perfect when it comes out of the gate.

The first year that I launched my Profit Acceleration Club for Entrepreneurs, not one person got a result. Did I quit? No. I went back. I looked at where the problem was. I surveyed my clients and asked them what would have helped them become successful. I went back to the drawing board, improved the program, relaunched it, sold more people into it, and had a better success rate. Today I have a 94 percent success rate in that program.

I share that with you because without that process, I would never have had the freedom or the income that the program allows me today. This foundation would never have been built, if I had tried to get it right on paper first and had not launched it until it was perfect.

The last bad habit common among entrepreneurs that I will discuss is their tendency to take on too many things at once. They do not focus on one thing all the way to the end.

Every month, my company has one focus. That one focus is something that everybody on the team—the admin staff, the accounting staff, the sales staff, the coaching staff, and me—is focused on.

One project might take up to three months, because you can focus for three months and knock something out of the park. However, it will never be longer than three months, because all the team members need a break to recover and refresh themselves so that they remain enthusiastic about what we do.

What I see happen all the time is that entrepreneurs are distracted by marketing campaigns online. It could, for example, be about video marketing. Then they think they have to learn how to do video marketing, because someone else just made $500,000 from such a campaign.

However, that is not the right way to develop your business. What you ought to do is build your business based on your plan and focus. Do not allow other things to distract you or take you off point. You cannot master everything. Focus on one thing, and master it to be a champion at running your company.

Some of your habits you must change to continue making more money. Other habits you need to keep. You cannot avoid making mistakes. However, do not stop investing, because risk tolerance is something you need as an entrepreneur. Be sure to invest in the right things at the right time, and stay focused all the way to the end.

THE BENEFITS OF ENDURANCE TRAINING

There are thousands of books about the topic of how to change habits. People have life-changing transformations when something drastic happens to them. It could be that somebody passes away, or they come down with a disease or illness. Dramatic events such as these make you shift momentarily, and you would hope it lasts a lifetime.

What I have found through research is that the act of training for races—triathlons, marathons, half marathons, etcetera—will reveal your habitual patterns. It will also help you change them faster and with more ease than anything else I have found. I cannot advise a bad habit out of you!

It is not a coincidence that many successful entrepreneurs and executives are people who run endurance races. Endurance is the key to seeing a plan all the way through. If you study successful people, you will notice that they have a lot of grit. Research the word *grit*. There are many books about it. I recommend *GRIT: The New Science of What It Takes to Persevere, Flourish, Succeed* by Dr. Paul G. Stoltz. It shows you four different areas of grit that you need to enhance: growth, resilience, instinct, and tenacity.

You need grit to start and fulfill a plan. It is the primary reason for success. It is difficult and takes many years to develop, unless you do something like endurance racing. Endurance racing is a little secret that a lot of successful people do.

Many miss this secret because they automatically put themselves in the category of not being an athlete. I was not an athlete either. I fell into endurance training. I started doing sprint triathlons and running half marathons that grew to more challenging races as I got stronger.

What I realized was that I had a three-day pattern. I would be on the third day of my commitment, and then something would happen that would cause me to change my schedule. If I were going to work out in the morning, I would change it to the evening. During the course of the week, I would eventually miss the workout. Then I looked at the way I was running my company and realized that I had a similar pattern.

There is a part of your brain that opens up when you do endurance sports, and a percentage of that you cannot access in other ways. It is not good enough to go to the gym or take spinning classes. You need to engage in an endurance sport. Grit comes with the endurance racing.

At HeartCore Business, we have a program called HeartCore Endurance. We teach people to train for races. About 2 percent of the participants are actual athletes. The rest of them are everyday entrepreneurs at different levels. They are closing their gaps and habits so that they can become better CEOs and more strategic and clear thinkers, and also grow their capacity to hold more!

Suzanne Evans is a good friend of mine, and she is also a mentor and coach. She participates in HeartCore Endurance. At the time of writing this book, Suzanne has a company that makes $7 million annually. I think she did it within about six years. You would think that Suzanne does not need endurance training, but she understands the importance of it. Recently, she posted a note in our Facebook group that said, "I just had my best live stream sales ever. Do you think it's a coincidence that I've worked out for 45 days straight?"

Even the most successful entrepreneurs have a gap that can be closed. They can always become better at what they do.

As I am writing this book, I am pregnant. Because of my pregnancy, I have gone from exercising twice a day to working out three days a week.

Because I reduced my training to three days a week, nothing in my company has grown—our workload has not increased. I have gained two to three work hours a day. However, I am the most overwhelmed, behind schedule, and foggy that I have been in three years since starting this lifestyle. I am now the bottleneck in my company. I need the endurance sports to think properly, make quicker decisions, and stay consistent, not to mention stay fit!

Do not think that more help is all you need to make your life easier. You need more than just help. You need to think differently. The way that you train for a marathon is the way to you run your business.

It is challenging to look at your business and admit that you need help. It is difficult to stop work at 5:00 p.m. and go to the gym, hang out with your loved one, or play with your children when there is a lot of work that must be done. It is a trap, because your business is connected to your survival and your self-worth. And you connect your identity with how you perform and how much money you make. Money is a measurement stick.

When you stop measuring yourself according to your performance at work and income, and instead measure your training for an endurance race, you will make wiser decisions, be more consistent, feel better, and look nicer. All of this impacts your energy as a leader. You start to solve problems differently, because you are out running instead of being in a meeting, preparing a presentation, or working on your computer. You get space and endurance to go all the way!

It changes how you think and grow your company. You can close the gap from the endurance training plan with less resistance than in your business because it is not connected to your survival or self-worth. The *effort* that you put into the training is what causes you to change the patterns and the habits of running your company.

It will help you close the mental gap. And when you can close the gap, that capacity spills over into how you run your company.

Say you are someone who commits but does not always follow through. When you participate in our HeartCore Endurance program, you train with a group of people. We have a professional athlete trainer who leads our HeartCore Endurance team. She gives group training rather than individual training because training in a group is more effective than individual training. When our entrepreneurs train together, they mix business and training, and they use the data to become better CEOs. When you train in a group, you become more consistent. And the positive effects of the training will start spilling over to your skills as a CEO.

Team accountability also creates consistency. When you read a post about an entrepreneur who takes a 22-hour flight to Asia and then goes for a run straight off the plane, it inspires you. If you had too much wine the night before and decided not to run, this example would help you get up and go for a run after all. The posts by other members of the group will help you close your gaps a lot more quickly and become more accountable to your goals. Money loves integrity and self-love. When you start putting yourself first, everything else starts to work.

Another thing that training for races does is create recognition for the entrepreneurs. After people run half marathons or marathons in Disneyland, they all receive medals, and they all wear them proudly. They do not make up the excuse that they are too fat, too slow, not athletes, cannot run, or hate running.

Amateurs want to feel passionate before they get started. Professionals know that they will feel passionate when they become good at something. Can you imagine when you transfer that skill to your business? What if you only did things you want to do in your company? If you are the kind of person who would not join something like an endurance program because you do not like running, I guarantee you that you operate like that in your business. You do what you want often, and you procrastinate doing the things you hate. Those are the filters and mindset that you make your decisions with in your business. You have to get rid of those habits. My reply to people who say they hate running is, "I don't care."

As entrepreneurs, we often have a hard time celebrating our success, and we are rarely given the recognition that we deserve. I give my staff flowers, chocolates, and thank-you cards to show them how I appreciate their efforts. I have received flowers from my staff maybe once in four or five years. I do not say that to criticize them. My point is that it is often lonely at the top. We need things that make us feel good about ourselves. We need things that give us recognition.

When you wear your medal at the end of a race, you walk around proudly. Oprah, actor Jim Carrey, inspirational teacher Eckhart Tolle, and most others who are at the top of their game are doing some kind of endurance sport.

There is a connection between endurance training and your capacity to make money, manage people, and avoid a burnout or a breakdown.

Changing your habits equals more success in your life. What are some of the habits that are costing you money and time? What do you need to do to close them? My suggestion is to join an endurance team.

Endurance sports help you increase your income level and decrease your stress level. Nicole is a client whom I have worked with for more than two years. I could not help her earn more than $5,000 per month. She had habits that caused her to start strong. We would give her a plan, but she would not do what it took to finish it.

She knew it, and it drove her nuts. She kept saying, "Shanda, why don't I finish the plan? I know what to do, but I just can't get myself to do it." My solution was to throw her into endurance sports. This was before I had started the HeartCore Endurance program. Within a couple of months, we jumped her income to about $12,000 a month. But then she got stuck and started falling into her old habits again.

Soon after, we opened up our endurance division where we started training a small group. The first group consisted of only 20 people. Since the training takes place virtually through conference lines, people from around the world come together and race, mostly in different parts of America.

When Nicole joined the endurance group and started training with the HeartCore Endurance team, she jumped to $30,000 recurring a month, and she worked part-time. I could never have talked that strategy into her.

So, you tell me: How long have you been trying to change your habit, and how amazing would it be if you could change it in three to four months and always reach your goals? That is what is possible.

♦

CHAPTER 12

LIVE A MEANINGFUL LIFE

We have covered a lot of ground in this book. At the end of the day, none of it means anything, unless you know what will make your life meaningful. Living a meaningful life is challenging. It should not be, but it is.

For many years, I used to say to others, and myself, that I was doing everything I did to be an amazing wife and an extraordinary mother. In my mind, family was what made wealth and an abundance of free time meaningful. However, I never prioritized to take the steps to have that meaningful life.

It is difficult to make the meaningful things a priority, because you always think you have to do something first to prepare for them.

It was not until I woke up one day that I realized, "Oh, my God, I'm almost forty years old, and I haven't had a child, and I'm not dating anyone." I was living a great life; I was traveling around the world and had more money than I could spend, but these pieces were missing. I would sometimes be at home watching Netflix and would feel moments of loneliness. Or I would be having a glass of wine and feel a strange underlying depression come over me. It was because striving to get more and be more only kept me occupied, not full!

Most people do not slow down because God forbid that they stop and get intimate with themselves and their lives. However, it is when you slow down or stop that you start to feel again. And when you start to feel again, you begin to realize that you need the key components that make your life meaningful. Answer this question: What would make your life feel amazing and full?

As I have said before, connection is currency. If we are not connected to other people, we lose our zest for life, and we cannot replace it with work.

The first things that we tend to neglect are the things that make our life meaningful, so let me caution you to put what is important to you above striving to make money. I have shown you how to schedule. I have shown you how to attract as many clients as you want. If you have challenges with selling, you can go to HeartCore Business and pick up our Cash Flow program. I have given you every resource that you need to make money, but I cannot make you create a quality life worth living. What I can do is bring it to your attention and urge you to put that first.

Creating a life worth living takes setting priorities. It takes strategy. It takes you being conscious so that you do not drop into a busy schedule. It requires you to have a calm and open mind. Some people meditate, which I think is phenomenal. I do that too. My favorite way to create an openness and space of mind is being physically active. Do not sacrifice special moments, your marriage, or your health to make money.

Making money and a meaningful life is not an either-or conversation. When I got together with my partner in life, Ash, I said to him, "Don't ever make me choose between you, our son, and my business, because I don't think in limitations."

I will always strategize a way to have it all. There are certain things of less importance that I sacrifice. For instance, I might not cook all my meals. I might have a chef bring them in. Though I love cleaning my house, I might not be the person who does it; I sacrifice that. I had to give up the mindset that I have to do everything to be valuable.

I used to think that I had to do it all. To be an amazing woman, I had to clean the house. I had to pack the lunches. I had to run a successful business. I had to be an extraordinary girlfriend to my girlfriends when they needed me. I had to do it all.

What happens with that mindset is that you develop a sense of resentment. For men, that resentment can often be that they pay for everything but they don't feel appreciated. For women, it often is that we do everything and don't feel appreciated. You are the only person who can prevent that dialogue from happening. You stop it by putting yourself first. When you put yourself above your children, your significant other, and your work, and you take care of yourself, you will have an overflow to take care of everybody else.

When you start running your schedule the way I have outlined in this book, you will realize that there is time to live a meaningful life, and it is on your terms.

Money and success love self-worth. I do not want you to read this book and then say, "Oh, it was a good book. It had me think about a few things," and then you go back to your old habits. I want you to take a few minutes, right now, to grab a piece of paper and answer these two questions.

1. What is important to me in my business?
2. What is important to me in my personal life?

Choose one thing in both areas. It is tempting to go down the rabbit hole and think that you cannot do it. Perhaps you are tempted to think that you are not good enough or you do not have the tools or the money to be able to live this out. Do not give in to that temptation.

If we fast-forwarded to the end of the year, what would make you feel successful and feel like you were living a quality life? Pick one thing in both your business and your personal life that would make you feel that way.

For me, that one thing in business would be to speak to 25,000 people in a stadium. If I could do that this year, I would feel like I had accomplished something extraordinary for myself. Regarding my personal life, if I could take one weekend every month this year and create an intimate family weekend with Ash and our son, I would feel like I am a good woman.

What is that for you at the end of this year? What two things are critically important to you? I know lots of ideas roll around in your head, but I urge you to limit yourself to two things.

When your mind is calm, do you focus and strategize a lot differently than when you try to accomplish a to-do list the size of Santa's Christmas list? Schedule your work to complement your life. Begin today. Tell everyone what you are doing. When I changed my work schedule to only working with clients Monday, Tuesday, and Wednesday morning, I told everyone. I told my friends, my family, my clients, and my staff that this is when I work with clients. It is non-negotiable. I am not asking them for permission or acceptance. I am telling them. I am leading my life and business.

Communication is your main focus. Once people know that you are only available on certain days for certain tasks, you train them how to treat you. Then people start reaching out to you at your scheduled times, and it is like the universe aligns with your vision. So, tell everyone what you are doing. And make a commitment to have an abundant life without sacrificing what is important to you.

Your core calling will not go away. You can be the person who never pays attention to it. You can be the one who makes up a million excuses for why you do not have the time or cannot focus on it at the moment. Then when you come down with an illness or something happens to you, and you realize you have lived out all your days, you will regret your choices. Or you can be spiritual and conscious. Then you realize that money, travel, power, love, or a more fit body is not what will make you happy and give you a meaningful life.

Happiness and a meaningful life come from first saying yes to yourself and manifesting your core calling.